Evolution and Consciousness

Contemporary Psychoanalytic Studies

Editor

Jon Mills
Adler Graduate Professional School, Toronto

Associate Editors

Gerald J. Gargiulo
Keith Haartman
Ronald C. Naso

Editorial Advisory Board

VOLUME 28

The titles published in this series are listed at *brill.com/cps*

Evolution and Consciousness

*From a Barren Rocky Earth to Artists,
Philosophers, Meditators and Psychotherapists*

By

Michael (Michelo) DelMonte and Maeve Halpin

BRILL
RODOPI

LEIDEN | BOSTON

Cover illustration: *Croagh Patrick Mountain in the Snow*, County Mayo, Ireland, by "Koert" Simeon Delmonte.

The Library of Congress Cataloging-in-Publication Data is available online at http://catalog.loc.gov
LC record available at http://lccn.loc.gov/2019945557

Typeface for the Latin, Greek, and Cyrillic scripts: "Brill". See and download: brill.com/brill-typeface.

ISSN 1571-4977
ISBN 978-90-04-40757-2 (hardback)
ISBN 978-90-04-40875-3 (e-book)

Printed by Printforce, the Netherlands

Contents

Foreword

Ivor Browne

A paradigm shift is taking place in the space where science and consciousness meet, revolutionising not just our understanding of the brain but also our perspective on meaning, purpose and our place in the universe.

The fixed, clockwork world of Galileo, Newton and Descartes is based on a worldview, or paradigm, which includes a fundamental split between mind and matter, seeing the physical universe as a soul-less, meaningless machine. This 400-year-old reductionist schism has plagued much scientific, medical and psychological thinking to this day.

Contemporary insights in the fields of systems theory, quantum physics, biology and genetics increasingly challenge these traditional views. Far from being a dead, pre-determined construction, the world is revealed as a fluid, dynamic, self-organising system driven by an innate intelligence that is evolving towards ever-greater complexity. As physicist Fritjof Capra describes it, we live in an interconnected, mindful, holistic universe that at the deepest level is beginning to look, metaphorically, more like music than solid matter.

1   The Systems Perspective

The 20th century brought the realisation that living creatures are open systems, both influencing and being influenced by their environments. In 1977, the chemist Ilya Prigogine was awarded the Nobel Prize for discovering the unique, non-deterministic qualities of self-organising systems. Perhaps his greatest achievement was to show that such systems were characterised by change, instability and continuous fluctuations. This indeterminacy reflected the radical findings of quantum physics at the beginning of the same century, when the unpredictability and immeasurability of sub-atomic particles undermined the previously unquestioned certainty of Newtonian physics.

In this spirit, the groundbreaking work of biologist Lynn Margulis challenges the neo-Darwinian orthodoxy of natural selection and the "survival of the fittest" model of evolution. Margulis argues that sym-biogenesis, involving inter-species co-operation more so than competition, is at the heart of how species evolve. Symbiosis among the first bacteria and archaea probably led to the evolution of cells with nuclei, and from there to other cellular organisms such as fungi, plants and animals. Margulis highlights how the concept of "the great chain of being", which places humans at the centre of the universe with the gods and angels above and the animals and plants below, obscures the essential co-equality and interdependence of all life on Earth. Gaia, the finely-tuned, largest ecosystem of the Earth's surface, is just symbiosis as seen from outer space.

In Chapter 1 of the current volume, psychologists Michael and Maeve unpack the limitations of a purely materialist approach to evolutionary theory and reflect on the ultimately mysterious emergence of the phenomenon of consciousness. The resonance of this new perspective for psychotherapy, as both client and therapist journey together towards healing and understanding, is explored.

Epi-genetics is another field which is throwing a critical light on everything we thought we knew about genetic inheritance. Since the discovery of DNA by Crick and Watson in 1957, the received wisdom has been that there is a relatively direct, linear relationship between our genes and their expression in observable traits, such as the physical development and behaviour of an organism. The relatively recent study of epi-genetics has shown that genes effectively interact with the whole organism and its environment, with external conditions causing certain genes to be "switched" on or off to varying degrees. Researchers in Sweden have also found evidence of environmental effects emulating epi-genetic patterns by being passed down several generations. This suggests that genes "behave" as if they have a form of "memory". Our genetic expression is therefore far more dynamic and environment-dependent than previously conceptualised.

The development of highly sophisticated technology for studying the brain has also led to a profound revision of neuro-scientific dogma. Only a few decades ago, it was assumed that the brain contained all of its neurones at birth: that they remained unchanged by life's experience and that no new brain cells are ever produced. Now, the proven ability of the brain to create new neuronal connections and to even generate entirely new neurones is referred to as "neuro-plasticity" or in colloquial terms, as the "plastic brain". For instance, the collaboration of neuroscientist Dr Richard Davidson with the Dalai Lama and his meditating monks has yielded rich new information on the physical changes in the brain brought about by meditation practice. The prefrontal cortex is related to the regulation of emotion. The left prefrontal cortex enhances positive emotions, whilst the right pre-frontal cortex tends to increase negative or destructive emotions. Rigorous testing of people who meditate regularly, compared with control groups, shows that meditation leads to a significant increase in left-sided brain activation.

Chapters Two and Three of this volume investigate the remedial qualities of meditation in terms of its role in transcending the mind/body, subject/object split that has bedevilled much of Western culture, and contributed to a pervasive sense of alienation and anxiety. The authors demonstrate the integrating and restorative experience of a regular meditation practice, often supported by psychotherapy, to be a profound path of personal growth. These practices can re-connect us with the ineffable, non-dual "ground of being", an undifferentiated sense of unity and oneness that many practitioners describe as a feeling of "coming home".

Our understanding of the emotions has also been transformed by a new awareness of the operation of the hormone ANF (atrial natriuretic factor), which is produced by the atrium of the heart. Because it interacts with other hormones, ANF has a controlling influence over the whole cardiovascular system and dramatically affects every major organ of the body. It has an impact on the limbic area of the brain, the thalamus, the pituitary gland and the pineal gland. These areas of the brain relate to our emotional life, learning and memory. It would appear that the heart is an important centre of our emotions, reflecting back on the brain. The many well-documented cases of recipients of heart transplants also "inheriting" the likes, dislikes and proclivities of their heart donors lends some anecdotal support to this view.

For the ancient wisdom traditions of the East, this is nothing new. Some of the first studies on compassion involved using electroencephalography (EEG) to study the brains of Tibetan monks who had for many years been practicing compassion or "loving-kindness" meditation. When the monks saw the skull-shaped EEG electrode caps that the researchers wanted them to wear, they laughed – not because the caps were funny, but, as one monk explained, "Everyone knows that compassion isn't in the head. It's in the heart."

2   Consciousness in Evolution

The development of life on Earth may appear at first sight to be directionless and chaotic. However, from a deeper perspective, it is significant that the evolution of ever more complex life forms has been accompanied by the emergence of the extraordinary phenomenon of consciousness. In fact, it is now becoming apparent that the more complex the interactions of any living system, the more "mind" appears to develop and the more conscious the system will become. Jesuit philosopher Pierre Teilhard de Chardin intuited this evolutionary trajectory, calling it "complexity-consciousness".

This emerging paradigm finds a deep resonance with the traditions of many indigenous people around the world who, as the work of biologist Elisabet Sahtouris demonstrates, understand science and spirituality as aspects of the same reality, an intelligent, conscious continuum with physical and non-physical aspects. Chapter 4 of this book considers the uniquely human capacity for symbolisation and how this can express a sense of the numinous and the sublime, revealing these transpersonal dimensions of existence.

The rich concept of the evolution of consciousness incorporates both the powerful insights of modern science and the deep wisdom of age-old cultures to affect a much-needed corrective synthesis of East and West, of the head and the heart, of male and female and of science and spirituality. To borrow a phrase from American philosopher Ken Wilber, it is a concept that "transcends and includes" all that has gone before. By integrating the benefit of diverse approaches it provides the world with an overarching and transcending model that moves us to a new level of meaning. In the current volume, Michael and Maeve explore the implications of these ideas in an accessible way, illustrating their significance for empirical research and their relevance to personal development and psychotherapy.

Preface

For most of its very long history, mother Earth was no more than a barren rock floating around in space with the other planets of our solar system. Somehow life evolved and later on, so did consciousness as we know it. Whilst our scientific understanding of the "how" of these remarkable unfoldings blossoms by the day, many metaphysical "why" questions still remain to ponder upon. Increasingly, emerging theories from diverse disciplines are focussing on the concept of evolution, seeing it not just as a biological phenomenon but also as a dynamic, multi-dimensional, and possibly a goal-directed process in which humans can increasingly participate.

In this volume, we distil and synthesise recent developments across a range of inter-related disciplines to present an integrated model of evolution. Advances in cognitive science, philosophy, psychology, systems theory, physics, astronomy and studies of consciousness inform our theorising. In the context of a broad, interdisciplinary approach, we interpret these exciting new findings for the inquisitive reader, illuminating their relevance to our psychotherapeutic journeys and to our perennial quest for meaning and purpose. As psychologists and psychotherapists we have a special interest in consciousness, as this is the very medium of our work.

Following the Introduction this book is divided into four self-contained chapters on evolution, constructivism, mindfulness and symbolisation respectfully. Although they are intentionally inter-related in that they all address the evolution and development of consciousness, they can be read as completely separate entities and in any chosen sequence. Nevertheless, they have been arranged in a developmental order from the Big Bang, the evolution of matter and of life, and onwards to subtler aspects of consciousness, culminating in the topic of symbolisation which is seen as an aspect of social consciousness. Psychodynamic, systemic and constructivist thinking permeates all parts of the book to varying degrees.

Acknowledgements

I wish to pay tribute to my late parents, Koert and Niesje, who sowed the seeds of existentialist enquiry into my youthful, but receptive mind. I would also like to show my gratitude to my dear wife, Patricia, and to my wonderful daughters, Nadja, Sonja and Anais, for their support and encouragement throughout the years while this book was being written.

Michael (Michelo) DelMonte

I am indebted to the trailblazing work on consciousness of William Irwin (Bill) Thompson, whose Lindsfarne talks I continue to find vital and transformative.

My family and friends have always non-judgementally supported me through all the vissitudes of life, including the writing of this book, for which I am eternally grateful.

Maeve Halpin

Introduction: The Evolution of Consciousness: a New Perspective on Our Search for Meaning

We are all familiar with the theory of biological evolution, which describes how the vast cornucopia of life on Earth evolved over millions of years, most likely from the "primordial soup" of ancient seas. It is estimated that life has been evolving on Earth for approximately 3.9 billion years. On this timescale, the gradual emergence of fully anatomically modern human beings is a relatively recent event, roughly estimated at approximately 300,000 years ago.

Biological evolution has no doubt slowly continued in human beings since that time, but the physical differences between human beings today and those of our ancestors of 300,000 years ago appear to be very slight. Essentially we are still the same human creatures today as then. But if we compare how we live today with how we lived then, we see an immense difference. The human story from the Palaeolithic, i.e., the Old Stone Age from about 2.6 million years ago, to the Neolithic, about 10,000 years ago, covered 95 percent of human technological history and was characterised by the use of very simple stone tools. Our more recent evolution into the modern world we know today has been less one of physical change, but rather a story of the evolution or development of human culture and consciousness. Some form of consciousness obviously exists at various levels throughout nature, but the reflective capacity for self-awareness, intelligence, imagination and creativity that emerged with humanity represents a unique and unprecedented leap forward in the evolution and complexity of consciousness on Earth. This was a major paradigm shift from the slow physical evolution of inorganic and organic matter to the relatively rapid evolution (or development) of mind and culture.

Human consciousness is, arguably, the defining characteristic of the human species; it is qualitatively what most distinguishes us from all the other species. Consciousness here is meant in the general sense of awareness, mind, cognition, will, intelligence and creative agency. The story of the evolution of human consciousness from the Palaeolithic to modern times is expressed in the development of human culture and civilisation, including technological, artistic and religious expressions. These sophisticated, highly evolved dimensions of our existence are what most distinguish Homo sapiens from other forms of life.

Just as ancient fossil records preserved in the geological rock strata are studied by evolutionary biologists, it is possible to follow and study the development of human consciousness in the archaeological, artifactual and historical records. These range from the stone implements, simple statuettes and cave paintings of the hunter-gathering societies of the Palaeolithic (up to about 10,000 years ago), to the pottery, earthen figurines and megalithic monuments of the farming communities of the Neolithic (up to about 4,000 years ago), to the temples, pyramids and irrigation systems of the great riverine civilisations of Mesopotamia, Babylon, Egypt, the Indus valley, China and elsewhere, on to our modern world of globalised technological civilisation. In short, we can trace the evolution of human consciousness through its manifestation as human culture, civilisation and technology.

Although there are many and evolving theories of consciousness, scientists have not yet reached a consensual understanding of how human consciousness arises or functions. But of one thing we can be absolutely certain: the immense power and impact of human consciousness on all forms of life on Earth and on the planet itself. The evolution of human consciousness has been described by some scientists and philosophers as the emergence of a "noosphere", or mind-sphere. The term noosphere was coined in the 1920s by a group of philosopher-scientists meeting in Paris, which included the Jesuit anthropologist Pierre Teilhard de Chardin and the Russian geochemist Vladimir Vernadsky. The word is borrowed from the French *noosphère*, which in turn is derived from the late Greek *noo-* (mind, intellect) and the French *-sphère* (sphere). The noosphere emerges through, and is constituted by, the interaction of human minds. Teilhard de Chardin and his colleagues argued that human consciousness and its product, human civilisation or the human world, represents an emerging new level of natural order on Earth. They believed that the human mind has become a force of "geological" proportion and power (Vernadsky, 1943/2005). They conceived of the noosphere as the third in a succession of phases of development during the Earth's history, following the geosphere (the mineral world) and the biosphere (the biological world).

We can see examples of the power of human activity affecting the planet in issues such as climate change, including the depletion of marine species due to industrial-scale fishing and pollution of the oceans. Human industrial civilisation is pumping vast quantities of carbon dioxide and other chemicals into the atmosphere, the seas and the soils at an annually accelerating rate. Many of the industrial effluents and chemicals are compounds which have never been in the biosphere prior to our times, so their long-term effects are unknown. The increasing incidence of extreme weather events around the world would appear to result from this disturbance of natural weather systems due, in large measure, to unsustainable human production, consumption and contamination of the biosphere and geosphere.

On a more positive note, the emergence of the Internet can be seen as the development of a technological "nervous system", integrating billions of individual human minds into an informational network that is increasingly catalysing both individual and global development. It is as if the planet itself has developed a brain. Most areas of human interaction, knowledge and creativity are being transformed and enriched by this global networking of information and sharing of ideas. The metaphor of the World Wide Web neatly captures the interrelated, transactional nature of the noosphere as a unifying field of consciousness. Teilhard de Chardin could be interpreted as foreseeing its appearance when he wrote in 1930 of "... the literally global physiology of an organism in which production, nutrition, the machine, research, and the legacy of heredity are, beyond any doubt, building up to planetary dimensions" (Teilhard de Chardin 1950/1978).

1   Models of the Evolution of Consciousness

> The adventure of awakening is among the most universal of human dramas.
>
> KEN WILBER, Integral Life Practice, 2008, p. 91

Our long evolutionary journey can be conceptualised as a progressive movement towards greater complexity, awareness and consciousness. As we have moved through the various stages of civilisation, creating and building the physical and socio-cultural structures which in turn shape us, we are participating in a reciprocal relationship which has brought us through a succession of major cultural shifts or transformations. The cycles of human history reveal that there have been relatively few of these, perhaps just half a dozen in our entire history. We appear to be on the cusp of one of these great transitional phases now, as we move from the industrial into the digital, globalised age.

A useful model for understanding the successive stages of cultural transformations in human history has been delineated by cultural historian and poet William Irwin Thompson (2001). These cultural transformations express the more recent evolution or development of human consciousness during the period since fully modern humans emerged approximately 300,000 BCE:

1   *Hominisation* = 4,000,000 to 300,000 BCE, when *Homo sapiens* evolved from earlier forms of hominid life.
2   *Symbolisation* = 300,000 BCE to 10,000 BCE, with the appearance of the first cave paintings, sacred objects and communal rituals.
3   *Agriculturalisation* = 10,000 BCE to 3,500 BCE, representing a shift from hunting and gathering to farming.

4   *Civilisation* = 3,500 BCE to 1,500 CE, the rise of cities.

5   *Industrialisation* = 1,500 CE to 1945 CE, marked particularly by the European Industrial Revolution, circa 1780 CE.

6   *Planetisation* = 1945 to present, a post-industrial, post nation-state, globalised, technological world. This stage requires a meta-system perspective. It is characterised by complex dynamical systems, a phrase that captures the interpenetration of multi-level systems that underlie and drive the evolution of our world. Global warming, for instance, has compelled us to recognise the implicate feedback loops embedded in such apparently diverse activities and systems as fossil fuel burning, consumerism, pollution, biodiversity, population growth, geo-politics and climate.

Thompson's framework provides a multi-layered overview of humanity as a progressive evolutionary system made up of a dynamic flux of individual and collective expressions of consciousness, moving towards ever-increasing complexity.

American philosopher Ken Wilber tracks how these cultural shifts are reflected in the emergence of successive philosophical worldviews (e.g. Wilber, 2000). Drawing on the ground-breaking work of Jean Gebser (1986) in relation to structures of consciousness, Wilber focuses on mental and intellectual evolutionary development, as evidenced in myth, religion and philosophical expressions. He identifies six distinct worldviews that have arisen from successive stages of consciousness over the ages. In practice many of these overlap and co-exist, contributing at times to "culture wars" among their adherents:

1   Archaic,
2   Magic (Tribal),
3   Mythic (Traditional),
4   Rational (Modern), including the Axial Age
5   Pluralistic (Postmodern),
6   Integral (Post-postmodern).

The *Archaic Stage of Consciousness* relates to our earliest appearance as humans, before self-awareness as we know it evolved. At this primeval level, consciousness is purported to be relatively undifferentiated, rather than individuated. At this stage humans do not have a sense of past and future, but live in a continuous present, with their direction and purpose rooted in instinct and survival. They have little experience of any separation from the natural world in which they are intimately embedded.

The *Magic Stage of Consciousness* evolved with language, with the first appearance of graven images, idols and rituals. The development of a rudimentary sense of self is being expressed through this first appearance of the use of symbols.

With the advent of tool making, the domestication of animals and the first very primitive lunar calendars about 35,000 years ago, *the Mythic Stage of Consciousness* appears. Humans at this stage are beginning to have a perspective on their separate existence, learning to manage nature through controlling fire, building shelters and weaving fibres. Creation myths from around the world are thought to date from this time. For instance, the expulsion of Adam and Eve from the Garden of Eden can be read as a metaphor for the losses of primeval innocence and harmony with nature, and with the emergence of the notion of gods that came with conscious self-awareness. The first couple's eating from The Tree of Knowledge resulted in The Fall, a transition from a state of naive and childlike obedience to one of rebellious knowledge and self-determination. The price they paid for choosing knowledge was their summary eviction from Paradise. This can be interpreted as "innocence is bliss"; but to grow, develop and evolve, we have to relinquish the bliss of immersive not-knowing and bear the suffering and alienation that questioning and individuality can bring. This is the burden of knowledge. The Mythic Stage of Consciousness represents this important juncture in our evolutionary journey

Between 10,000 B.C. and 500 B.C a radical shift took place – the development of *Rational Consciousness*. The development of rationality, particularly an understanding of cause and effect, marked the beginning of humans' capacity for reflection, abstraction, philosophy and scientific thinking. This laid the foundations for scientific objectivity and investigation and for individual achievement. This shift represents the genesis of the noosphere, the world of higher systems created by the collective activity of human minds. This includes the fields of technology, science, law, education, literature and so on.

The period 800 BCE to 200 BCE has been called the Axial Age in that it represented a fundamental shift in human consciousness, with a unique flowering of philosophy, theology and the questioning of old certainties. China, India, Persia, Mesopotamia, Greece and the Mediterranean in general saw a simultaneous upsurge of spiritual originality and creativity, with the appearance of great sages and theoretical systems that still influence human culture and thought today. Buddhism, Jainism, Taoism, Zoroastrianism, Judaism and Indian philosophy (e.g. the Upanishads) all emerged during this period. Greece produced a whole spectrum of philosophical and creative activity in the works of Homer, Heraclitus, Socrates, Plato, Aristotle, Aeschylus, Sophocles, Euripides and a host of others. In China, this was the time of Confucius and Lao Tzu, the founder of Taoism, as well as several schools of Chinese philosophy, while the great Jewish prophets including Amos, Isaiah, and Jeremiah appeared in the Middle East. Christianity and Islam were to emerge later from Judaism.

> What is new about this age, in all three areas of the world, is that man becomes conscious of Being as a whole, of himself and his limitations. He experiences the terror of the world and his own powerlessness. ... All this took place in reflection. Consciousness became once more conscious of itself, thinking became its own object.
>
> JASPERS, 1953, p. 2.

The development of rationality also underpinned the gradual unfolding of the modern scientific world, starting in the Arab Islamic Empire and Moorish Spain a millennium ago, on to the European Renaissance (14th–16th centuries) and the later Enlightenment (17th–18th centuries), followed by the Industrial Revolution (18th–19th centuries). The seeds of our modern, secular, technologically advanced society were sown in the advent of the rational world view, representing a break from the mythical perspective to a more objective, analytical and experiential approach to understanding the world.

The next stage or level, *the Pluralistic Stage of Consciousness,* is the basis of postmodern values. Truth is seen as socially constructed and therefore relative, with no absolutes existing in any domain. If meaning is to be found, it can only be at the level of the individual, who is tasked to interpret the world and its symbols in whatever way has most resonance for him or her. Whilst this phase has been interpreted by many as a nihilistic, superficial cultural desert, it also has proved to be a fertile ground for the deconstruction of traditional, received ideas and the emancipation of individual creativity and self-expression.

Gebser and Wilber suggest that we are now on the threshold of a new phase, that of *the Integral Stage of Consciousness.* This incorporates and transcends all previous stages, acknowledging the unique value of each, while integrating and synthesising them. At this stage of consciousness, humans move beyond egocentricity and identification with their groups (e.g. nationality, religion or ethnicity) and perceive the interdependence and unity of all sentient beings within a living ecosystem. This consciousness is motivated and fed by a universal, non-discriminating empathy and compassion which sees beyond superficial differences and embraces diversity, equality and spirituality. Many people at this level of consciousness are aware of multiple dimensions of existence beyond the physical, experiencing a connection to others and to the planet that rises above individual narcissism, as well as beyond tribal and national divisions, which are forms of extended narcissism.

Other writers such as Barbara Marx Hubbard (2015), Clare Graves (2005) and Elisabet Sahtouris (2000) have similarly developed models of evolution that see us moving from the relative unconsciousness of the animal world to the self-awareness of language, symbolisation, religion and civilisation, towards a transcendent post-egoist consciousness based on compassion, wisdom and reciprocity, as articulated by the sages of all eras.

These evolutionary stages reflect a dialectical relationship between consciousness and culture, each influencing the other in an ongoing, reflexive feedback loop. The many scholars, artists, visionaries and mystics over the centuries who were considered "ahead of their time" were often people whose level of consciousness had advanced further than that of their culture, leaving them misunderstood, often persecuted, or ignored until well after their lifetimes. Consciousness has now become conscious of itself and humans are participating in their own evolutionary growth through myriad means of self-development, education, cultural participation and various psycho-spiritual disciplines and practices. For instance, the Buddhist monk Thich Nhat Hanh has coined the term "inter-being" to describe the interconnectedness and interdependence of all earthly systems (Nhat Hanh, 1987).

2   The Goal of the Journey

> The opposite of a fact is a falsehood, but the opposite of one profound truth may well be another profound truth
> Physicist and Nobel Laureate, NIELS BOHR (1885–1962)

The integral perspective includes the important insight that humans function at all levels at different times in their personal development and under different conditions of life and experience. For individuals, the evolutionary journey involves becoming more conscious of the level of our functioning in any moment or situation. This allows us to become more aware of how our thoughts and actions affect ourselves and others, both positively and negatively. In this way we can take responsibility for developing our own awareness and sensitivity, while accepting and valuing the many and diverse approaches and worldviews that differ from our own.

Whilst employing different models and viewing the evidence through different lenses, what evolutionary theorists do agree on is that consciousness is developing or evolving towards greater awareness, insight, reflexivity, imagination and sophistication of expression.

Using different metaphors and practices, the wisdom traditions such as Buddhism, Taoism and Hinduism, to list but a few, would assert that most of us, if not all of us, have the intrinsic potential to achieve the evolutionary summit of enlightenment, as attained by the Buddha himself, as well as by many Buddhist and Hindu sages – although they may argue that this could take many re-incarnations!. Enlightenment refers to an attainment of wisdom and clarity that signals a release from the suffering of everyday existence into a state of greater awareness and freedom from greed, hatred and delusion.

For integral theorists such as Wilber, the trajectory of our evolution is towards a holistic, expansive, all-encompassing understanding that rises above apparent divisions and unites people in a common cause. This transcends and includes all previous stages, drawing on the best from each. Integral consciousness is manifested through people living with integrity, wisdom and compassion, thereby inspiring co-operation, dialogue and conflict resolution in society at large.

3   Evolution and Consciousness: an Incredible Journey

> The scientist, the philosopher, the saint and the artist, all take different paths up the mountain, but the higher up they go, the closer they come together at the peak of human consciousness. Each is given the grace of a different landscape on the way up, but one landscape is not better than the other.
> WILLIAM IRWIN THOMPSON, 1981, p. 82

We "swim" in a world of apparent, everyday reality, but often sense a deeper, ultimate Reality, just ourside of our perception. Scientists, philosophers and spiritual seekers attempt to glimpse ultimate reality through different "windows", their differing insights all contributing to our collective knowledge base.

The current volume synthesises a number of diverse perspectives to illustrate how our individual experience can both reflect and contribute to the evolution of consciousness, at personal, social and cultural levels. The ultimately mysterious phenomena surrounding the evolution of life and consciousness are explored in the context of the ongoing evolution of our physical universe itself. The complexity of life-forms that evolution produces has increased over time, beginning with single-celled organisms such as microbes and amoebae and culminating in the extraordinarily high-level intricacy of the human body and brain.

The development of consciousness through language and other forms of symbolisation is examined in the context of psychodynamic and constructivist theories of the mind. The role of meditation and mindfulness in enhancing and expanding consciousness and a capacity for symbolisation is explored. The subtle and powerful connection between the mind and the body is considered, with the work of psychotherapy seen as healing the psychological splits that lead to debilitating psychosomatic and other symptoms.

In this light, the psychotherapist can be thought of as a midwife of personal evolution, helping clients to move beyond their relative unconsciousness and subliminal distress patterns. Suffering can be transformed into awareness, compassion, empathy, more accurate and conscious symbolisation, and ultimately, a wider and deeper appreciation of the wonder of life.

The Evolution of Matter and Mind

1   Introduction

Our solar system, including our Earth, is about 4.5 billion years old. About 3.8 billion years ago, life appeared on Earth (Reeves, 2005, 2011; Harari, 2014). Thus for nearly a billion years, the Earth was a barren assembly of inorganic minerals and rocks floating around in space with its "daughter" the Moon in orbit. Somehow, life evolved from matter, eventually leading on to the development of human consciousness. There are many "why" and "how" questions apropos the "causes" of this remarkable evolution. Whereas "how" questions are best addressed scientifically, "why" questions, on the other hand, merit metaphysical and philosophical consideration. Reflecting on both the "how" and "why" of evolution can deepen our understanding of the context of psychotherapy and of the deeper meaning of psychological health and wellness for clients.

The Darwinian theory of evolution, emphasising ecological adaptation, natural selection and "survival of the fittest" is undoubtedly one of the most influential and compelling theoretical models of our time. However, when we look at life solely through the lenses of mainstream evolutionary theory, then diverse cultural phenomena such as music, painting, philosophy, poetry, literature, mathematics, architecture, etc., are envisaged as mere by-products of the complex workings of human brains which purportedly developed via "blind evolution" (Dawkins, 1976). Put differently, human life and all its cultural manifestations are an "accident" of bio-chemical evolution and have no *a priori* meaning *per se*. With this radical materialist model, there is an implied primacy of matter over mind, i.e. the human mind is an epi-phenomenal outgrowth of matter, having no existence or meaning outside of our biological evolution on Planet Earth. Moreover, from Dawkins's neo-Darwinian perspective, spiritual values are just social meme-correlates and like all other cultural memes, are purely functional and are thus devoid of any intrinsic value as such (Hogan, 2008).

One does not have to be a literal believer in Biblical Creationism or even in Intelligent Design to question the above simplistic view. Creationism and Intelligent Design tend to represent the origins of the universe in terms of creation by a Judeo-Christian God, referencing biblical sources. They usually date the origin of the universe to about 6,000 years ago, based on deduction from the Book of Genesis, the first Book of the Old Testament. As we know this date

is incorrect, it would appear that these sources are better understood symbolically and metaphorically, rather than literally, which may never have been the
intention in the first place.

Thus without turning to a scriptural interpretation, evidence from numerous disciplines leads us to reflect on the limitations of the purely materialist
view of life. Theorists in fields as diverse as systems theory, quantum physics,
biology, ethnography, consciousness studies and psychology are challenging
materialist assumptions so as to develop a richer, more integrated theory of
mind that corresponds to people's everyday subjectivity and satisfies our need
for a more holistic and comprehensive explanation of the human experience.

Chapter 1 of this book briefly explores the phenomenon of the evolution
of matter and life since the "Big Bang", situating psychotherapeutic theory
and practice today in the context of evolutionary theory, and in the current
Zeitgeist of a growing confidence in genetics, biochemistry, neuroscience
and, by implication, in evolutionary psychology. Our long evolutionary journey out of inorganic matter, up to the complex world we live in today, pos-
es many challenging questions. It is contended that Darwinian Theory and
random mutations can only offer a partial explanation of human behaviour
and psychopathology and that broader considerations must also inform our
theorising. A synthesis of radical new insights across a range of disciplines
will demonstrate that consciousness itself is central to developing a coherent model of mind. The perspectives of the transcendent and transpersonal,
which appeared to have been lost in 20th century secular materialism, are
re-emerging in diverse scientific areas as researchers explore the complexity
and interdependence of life on Earth. These endeavours are discussed in a
very broad context by drawing on the laws of physics, as well as on genetic,
ethological, geo-physical, psychodynamic, constructivist, systemic, Eastern
and Western philosophical considerations.

We begin Chapter 1 by addressing our quest for understanding and meaning.
Then we go on to compare proximate (or lifetime) factors with distal (or evolutionary) factors. This sets the stage for addressing the mind/matter debate in
an evolutionary context. In this debate, dualists contend that mind and matter,
or mind and body, are separate, with mind emerging late in our evolutionary
journey. Monists on the other hand, maintain that there is just one underlying "substance" from which everything, both mind and matter, emanate. For
example, in Neo-Platonism, as expounded by the 3rd century Greek Plotinus,
everything is derived from "The One" and from it, manifest life unfolds to ever-
increasing levels of complexity (O'Brien, 1964).

The question of causality is central to this debate – which comes first, what
causes what? The traditional position on causality is linear – cause and effect

can only go in one direction. Either mind results from matter, or vice versa. The growing field of systems theory, which sees an embeddedness and interrelatedness in the implicate order that underlies the known world (e.g. Bronfenbrenner, 2005) challenges this naive assumption. The implication of this for the theory and practice of psychotherapy is drawn out, as the basic, often unconscious, assumptions with which we work will inevitably influence our interactions and interventions with clients. Becoming conscious of what we bring to the work as therapists will, hopefully, allow us to work more authentically and effectively with clients.

2   Methods of Inquiry: the Search for Meaning

The search for meaning is a uniquely human endeavour which distinguishes us from other forms of life. The current unprecedented advances in science, technology and communications have contributed much to our quality of life, but largely leave the deeper, existential questions of meaning untouched.

Scientists typically endeavour to uncover "the truth" by obliging nature to reveal her "hidden" secrets to us. This "internalist" method of inquiry (Langs and Badalamenti, 1996) in which we "dissect" the material objects of our world – be they mineral, vegetable or human matter – so that we come to understand them better, has its undoubted merits, especially when dealing with the "how" questions involved in investigating the objective world. All of modern science and technology has developed out of this rationalistic, objective scientific methodology.

However, this approach also has its limitations, particularly when it comes to understanding consciousness and the meaning of human subjective experience. With "how" (or scientific) questions, we take objects apart in order to investigate their constitutive parts. On the contrary, with "why" questions we assemble our observations in order to construct holistic, systems-based meaning.

Distinctions have thus been made between the scientific, or Logical Positivist (Comte, 1855), method of inquiry typical of the natural sciences on the one hand and the qualitative methods of the human sciences on the other (Oatley, 1992; Brewin and Andrews, 1997; DelMonte, 1997). Whereas the natural sciences deal with the (objective) mechanistic and non-intentional domain, i.e., the domain of "hard" facts, the human sciences are mainly concerned with (subjective) goals, plans and intentions (Brewin and Andrews, 1997). They also address meaning and the "why" domain.

Comprehensive meaning is ultimately *holistic* and cannot simply be deduced reductively from just one perspective, e.g. solely from the biological domain. Meaning is more likely to be contextual, i.e. systemic. Systems Theory (von Bertalanffy, 1968) and Dynamic Systems Theory (Clark, 1997; Gaussen, 2001) go beyond simple "internalism" to embrace context, taking the extra-psychic and the inter-psychic domains into consideration when attempting to arrive at understandings of the human condition. A radical contextual approach should, ideally, endeavour to include all major domains of investigation in attempting to comprehend our experiences – that is, encompass the inorganic, the biological, the psychological, the social and, for some, even the spiritual and cosmic domains. This integral, all-inclusive approach is becoming increasingly popular as access to knowledge becomes democratic and globalised and the distinctions between the disciplines become more permeable (e.g. Thompson, 1981).

3   Evolutionary Psychopathology

It has been postulated (Brown, 2002) that causation should be seen as a *relational* process which can exist in the dimensions of both space and time. The recent upsurge of interest in evolutionary psychopathology is a welcome attempt to extend chronologically the scope of our investigations into past influences on psychological disorders encountered today (Stevens and Price, 1996; Gilbert, 1998a). This evolutionary approach, which looks to the past to explain the present, is another valid aspect of aetiology or the origins of illness.

Ontogeny is the development of an individual throughout his or her lifespan, i.e. from conception onwards. It implies an interaction between a given genotype (genetic constitution), and its changing environment, to produce an unfolding phenotype (observable characteristics). Most psychological theorising, as in behaviourism, cognitive therapy and psychoanalysis, emphasises the importance of the ontogenetic, or life-cycle, factors in psychopathology. Here psychopathology is seen to be due to an individual's life-events impacting on a developing phenotype with a particular genotype.

Whilst most theorists accept the importance of proximate (i.e. ontogenetic) causes to psychopathology, others have strongly argued that evolutionary, that is distal, factors should not be overlooked (Stevens and Price, 1996; Gilbert, 1998a; Nesse, 1998). Darwinian Theory is applied to argue that, phylogenetically, many psychiatric and psychological disorders can be explained as evolving in past (often harsher) environments which at the time afforded them a selective advantage in certain contexts, e.g. paranoia, anxiety and phobia can be understood as having survival value where serious conflict and danger really existed.

Research into, and direct observation of, animal behaviour provides a supportive ethological underpinning to these claims (Dixon, 1998). Many forms of psychopathology have been investigated and analysed from a phylo-genetic and/or ethological perspective. Thus, current maladaptive behaviours, attitudes and disorders may represent the activation of previous (i.e. paleo-ethological) adaptive strategies (Gilbert, 1998a). Many detailed examples have been given and these include depression (Price and Gardner, 1995; Gilbert, 1995; McGuire and Troisi, 1998; Nesse, 1998 Thwaites and Dagnan, 2004; Carey, 2005); manic-depressive or bi-polar mood disorders (Wilson, 1998; Price, 1998); eating disorders (Abed, 1998; Troop et al., 2003; Faer et al., 2005), as well as a whole range of emotional states and disorders including shame, guilt, anxiety, panic, anger, social phobia, agoraphobia, hypochondriasis, acrophobia, paranoia, schizoid personality, dependent personality, sado-masochism, etc. (Stevens and Price, 1996; Gilbert, 1998a; Dixon, 1998; Nesse, 1998). Cognitive biases, cognitive distortions, social manipulation and psychological defences have also been described and analysed from the perspective of evolutionary bio-psychology, whereby their selective usefulness in terms of survival fitness is highlighted (Dixon, 1998; Gilbert, 1998b; Gardner, 1998). For example, a depressive presentation may not only fend off further attack when one feels socially demoted or defeated, but may also attract rehabilitative social support.

Moreover, the evolutionary perspective is not just confined to explaining current psychopathology. It is likewise used to describe the adaptive advantages of social co-operation and communication (Bailey and Wood, 1998; Gardner, 1998; Price, 1998; Gilbert, 1998b; Dixon, 1998; Cavalli-Sforza, 2000). It is claimed, for example, that submissive behaviour can be prompted by fear of harm to oneself, or even by a concern for emotional harm to others by presenting oneself as unthreatening (O'Connor et al, 2000). In the context of group-living, reciprocal altruism would facilitate survival. Inequity guilt, following one's own relative success, could trigger the kind of submissive behaviour which wards off envious attacks. However, evolutionary theory has been used to explain eating disorders from quite opposing, and thus contradictory, perspectives, namely as a sign of submissive behaviour (Troop et al., 2003) and also as female competition for mates and status (Faer et al., 2005).

4   Consciousness and Learning

Darwinian Theory has also been invoked to account for the emergence of conscious cognition, in that the evolution of consciousness in the direction of free will, as seen in humans, may have survival selective value (Lindahl, 1997;

Arhem and Liljenstrom, 1997). But how did this come about? Phylogenetic or evolutionary "learning" may lead to the type of knowledge that organisms use in unconscious processes as found in homeostasis, sleep cycles, immune responses, body maintenance, temperature regulation, biological "clocks" and organ repair. It can be argued that such learning has accumulated over numerous generations via natural selection. Phylogenetic learning is thus slow but relatively accurate in terms of environmental fit.

On the other hand, ontogenetic learning, or life-span, developmental learning, is less accurate but relatively fast. Ontogenetic learning delivers the more conscious type of knowledge gathered over the life-time of an organism. Phylogenetic or long-term knowledge is akin to Immanuel Kant's "a priori knowledge", and life-time traditional learning (ontogenetic knowledge) is akin to Kant's "a posteriori knowledge" (Arhem and Liljenstrom, 1997). Basically, phylogenetic knowledge (genetic "memory") can be seen to be based on Darwinian natural selection. This a priori knowledge dominates over the a posteriori knowledge acquired during our life cycles, with the whole organism being sculptured by phylogenetic learning.

Popper (1959) claimed that 99% of our knowledge is a priori. It is all unconscious – and so is most of our a posteriori knowledge. Only a small part of our ontogenetically acquired a posteriori knowledge is conscious (Arhem and Liljenstrom, 1997). Thus, conscious knowledge, although impressive, is still only a very small fraction of total knowledge. For Schwartz (2000), only between 1% and 5% of mental functioning is conscious. Thus, it has been argued, most of our knowledge is unconscious. It probably is not required for much of ordinary day to day functioning.

This unconscious knowledge appears to be akin the "archetypal" knowledge of Jung's "collective unconscious" (Jung, 1958b). However, we humans can have various experiences of expanding our consciousness. This can be achieved by bio-feedback when we learn to control aspects of our physiological functioning such as skin temperature, brain-waves, blood pressure, muscle tension and the like. Mindfulness meditation helps us to become more aware of the contents of our minds and of the social reality in which we are embedded. We can also make aspects of the repressed unconscious conscious through various types of dynamic psychotherapy. These issues are addressed later in much more detail.

5   Ultimate Causes

Darwinian Theory has, over the years, had great intellectual appeal, feeding the imagination of many theorists and clinicians. For example, Sigmund

Freud's "drive theory" and "seduction hypothesis", as well as John Bowlby's work on attachment behaviour, were ultimately inspired by Darwinian Theory (Mitchell, 1998). Freud's notion of "archaic vestiges" and Carl Jung's views on "archetypes" can also be traced back to evolutionary theory. Socio-biology was also hatched in the Darwinian cradle. It can even safely be argued that B.F. Skinner's behaviour theory was, somewhat surprisingly, in the grasp of evolutionary theory. His book, *"Beyond Freedom and Dignity"*, argued that between genetic determination and environmental conditioning there is no real free will (Skinner, 1971). Harari (2015) agrees with Skinner that there is no free will because humans are governed by their "biological algorithms", which in turn are determined by the interaction between their genes and the environment.

One cannot dispute the impact of Darwinian Theory on psychological discourse and clinical practice (Plomin, 2001). This was especially true in its birthplace (class-stratified, mercantile and worldwide colonial 19th century Great Britain) from whence it spread, especially to the (now) English-speaking parts of the world and gradually beyond. Its explanatory power was, and still is, appealing and, for some, seductive. The view of the 'survival of the fittest' provided an apologia for European colonial domination. It was also enthusiastically embraced by the 'Young Turks' in the early 20th century, and later by Nazi apologists in their genocidal attempts to eliminate Armenians and Jews respectively, as well as others considered to be 'inferior'. Apart from a period after the Second World War, confidence in Darwinian Theory grew and grew, so much so that phylogenetic (i.e. distal) factors are now being described as the "ultimate" cause of human behaviour and pathology (McGuire and Troisi, 1998; Abed, 1998). This suggests that phylogeny ultimately explains ontogeny, i.e., our evolutionary history dominates our personal developmental journey.

Is this a step too far, too simplistic? Can we really equate "ultimate" causes with natural selective forces operating in the past? In this volume, we prefer the term "distal causes" to "ultimate causes". Darwinian Theory is increasingly being invoked to account for all human behaviour, e.g. by Richard Dawkins (2006) who stated that the "natural selection" of genes "explains the whole of life" (p.116) – thus including consciousness. Like Birtchnell (1995), we would also prefer to exercise some caution when applying simple animal models to humans. Moreover, we would like to go further and question the hypothesis that evolutionary forces, in the strict Darwinian sense, are unquestionably the "ultimate" causes of all of our behaviours – be they instinctive, social, cultural or spiritual.

In brief, we are questioning the view that "ultimate causes" are solely bio-aetiological. Why exclude teleological considerations, i.e. the questions of purpose or meaning? According to the *Concise Oxford Dictionary* "ultimate" implies "last, final, beyond which no other (cause) exists or is possible". Ultimate causes (i.e. Aristotelian "*Causes Finales*") cannot exclude teleology, which according to the same dictionary is the "doctrine of final causes, a view that developments are due to the purpose or design that is served by them". The concept of teleology originated in the writings of the pre-Christian Greek philosophers Plato and Aristotle. The Greek word "*telos*" implies "end or purpose", and "*logos*" in Greek suggests "reason". Is phylogenetic backward elaboration in the search of explanatory "reason" sufficient?

In contrast to the British thinkers, early European philosophers (with their "Continental" perspective) had tended to see evolution more in Platonic idealist terms using logic and reason, rather than from the British "adaptationist" and "analytic" philosophical perspective (Kohn, 2004). The "adaptationist" perspective is closely related to the Darwinian theory of natural selection, in so far as this phenomenon implies an adaptation to the environment. This "Analytic" philosophical perspective has much in common with Comte's (1855) Logical Positivist scientific position already referred to above. In so far as one assumes, with Logical Positivism, that the whole of reality can be understood solely from a biological, empirical and scientific perspective, it can be described as a form of "naïve realism", which suggests that the senses alone provide us with a direct and reliable awareness of the external world. This naive realism perspective assumes a high correspondence between our sensory perceptions and ultimate reality. But is apparent reality, as mediated by our senses, adequate in attempting to know ultimate reality?

6   Is Evolution Really Blind?

Clearly the phenomenon of evolution is not at all being disputed here, but only its "causes". The abundance of geological, anatomical, genetic and fossil evidence supporting evolution does not necessarily imply that Darwinian Theory can account for all of it.

Is the evolution of life really "blind" as Dawkins (1976) has contended – heading nowhere in particular? Why have the inorganic atomic elements also evolved with increasing complexity in solar "furnaces" after the Big Bang? Is it an innocent co-incidence that matter, like life, has also evolved in complexity – yet all of this is purportedly heading nowhere?

Evolution is multi-faceted. It is not just confined to life forms such as plants and animals, but also, prior to that, to physical matter and more recently to the realm of ideas. This "mental" evolution had to be preceded by the evolution of consciousness itself, and then by the production, selective survival and spread of useful mental concepts (also called "memes" by Dawkins). There also appear to be cultural, ethical, moral and spiritual components to relatively recent evolution. Thus evolution can take place at various levels, from the inorganic concrete level right up to higher levels of abstraction. Let us go back to the beginning. Why does anything exist at all?

7   **The Evolution of Matter**

With what has become to be known as the "Big Bang" circa 13.7 billion years ago, four-dimensional time and space as we know them, supposedly, started from so-called "point zero" (Gribbin, 1999; Reeves, 2005). "Point zero" therefore represents a theoretical point of infinite density and of infinite gravity, without time or space, prior, to the "Big Bang" from which everything emerged. In this respect point zero is akin to a Black Hole. At the time of the Big Bang all the energy of our current vast universe existed already as *potential* energy, because, according the First Law of Thermodynamics, energy can neither be created nor destroyed. However, this potential energy can change form, i.e. into matter or into several different types of energy such as the chemical, mechanical, kinetic, solar or thermal energy that we now find on Earth.

Thus energy and matter supposedly came into being *ex-nihilo* ("creation from nothing"), but possibly from pre-existing minuscule quantum particles to form an extremely dense, homogenous and hot "plasmic primordial soup" in a rapidly expanding universe (cosmic inflation), which gradually became less dense and less hot (Al-Khalili and McFadden, 2014; Al-Khalili, 2016, 2017). Equal amounts of matter and anti-matter should have formed but then cancelled each other out. Luckily, there is much more matter than anti-matter – thus our physical universe exists! Only about three minutes after the Big Bang, the first sub-atomic nuclei appeared, primarily neutrons and protons, by a process known as "Big Bang nucleosynthesis". Atoms spontaneously formed 380,000 years after the Big Bang from these sub-atomic particles. These positively charged sub-atomic particles "trapped" negative electrons to form atoms, and thus visible light also appeared for the first time in our universe.

Hydrogen was the first atomic element to form in this, by then relatively cold, primitive universe. It remains the most prevalent element in our universe at 74 percent of all elements. Subsequent nuclear fusion led to the formation of helium (24 percent) and to a little lithium and beryllium, in that order. These four atomic elements went on to form the hot stars. With a couple of exceptions, all the other atomic elements (only 2 percent of the total) were later forged by thermo-nuclear fusion in extremely hot solar furnaces in a process which continues to this day called "stellar nucleosynthesis". These forged elements were ejected into inter-stellar space by dying giant stars. In all, 92 naturally occurring atomic elements evolved over time. However, today there are 118 atomic elements in all, as several man-made ones have been forged. The naturally occurring elements became the matter and energy of our universe, and thus subsequently the "building blocks" of our world.

With this Big Bang (there may have been prior ones) our universe began to evolve in complexity from (almost?) nothing. Following the laws of physics, chemistry, mathematics, etc (i.e., the fundamental Laws of Nature), it began to take form, including our galaxy (one of billions) with its billions of solar systems – each with their own sun, planets and moons. On our Earth, which formed about 4.5 billion years ago, forms of life of increasing complexity and eventually with a consciousness, capable of reflecting upon the Big Bang itself, emerged. What was happening during those billion years to allow life and consciousness to emerge on the Earth?

8   The Emergence of Life on Earth

When we talk about the origin of life (biogenesis) we normally have in mind its biological beginnings and manifestations on Earth. It has been argued that simple organic matter, like carbon dioxide or methane, or even very primitive forms of life, could have been "seeded" by asteroids, meteorites or comets falling onto Earth from extra-terrestrial sources. This suggestion is known as "panspermia" (Wickrama-Singh, 2001). Alternatively, simple organic compounds carried on comets crashing into Earth at very high speed could have been converted into amino acids due to the enormous energy released on impact. Amino acids are the building blocks of proteins, and proteins are essential to living organisms. Moreover, comets landing on Earth probably did deposit large amounts of water, which would have facilitated the evolution of life.

The public position held by many, if not most, scientists (e.g. Maynard Smith, 1966; Reville, 1996) is that life eventually emerged on Earth as the result of chemical evolution, i.e. inorganic chemicals such as minerals, increased in complexity and "somehow" became organic. This process is known as "abiogenesis" – the apparently spontaneous emergence of simple organic life from inorganic matter. For example, it may be that life evolved in deep seawater in hot hydro-thermal vents, as under these high pressure and very hot conditions, carbohydrates seem to appear spontaneously. Did either lightning storms impacting on water or erupting volcanoes and volcanic hot springs have similar life promoting effects? Volcanic hot pools around hot springs could be a possible cradle for the emergence of life on Earth. Alternatively, it may be the case that life emerged deep below the Earth's surface, i.e. intra-terrestrially, where, due to favourable pressure and temperature conditions, we find an abundance of microbial life today. Maybe one day all these speculations may be resolved.

There is little or no disagreement that hydrogen, the first, simplest and the most abundant of the atomic elements, evolved into more complex atomic elements via nuclear fusion. These atoms in turn eventually fused to become simple molecules, which in time evolved into complex molecules such as found in minerals. However, it is further argued that certain, essential to life, carbon compounds arose "by chance", and gradually developed or evolved into more complex chemicals capable of self-replication. We humans are also formed from the same atomic elements as found in the rest of the universe. It is the way these atoms are structured and organised together that makes all of the difference. New properties emerge out of increasing structural complexity. But why should chemicals evolve in complexity by chance, or rather, from where did the laws of chemistry hail?

Just how the simpler inorganic elements evolved into more complex atoms and molecules, and how ordinary inorganic matter became animated by a "life-force" that distinguishes living matter from inanimate chemical matter, is still largely unknown. Likewise, the question as to why this vital animation should have occurred at all leaves scientists guessing.

Whatever their origins, it is accepted that very simple virus-like life-forms (prokaryotes) appeared on Earth about 3.9 billion years ago, i.e. less than a billion years after the Earth was formed. It took about another two billion years for single-celled eukaryotic life to emerge, with cell structures similar to that of the plant and animal life found today. Next, multi-celled eukaryotic life evolved, setting in train the slow evolution of multi-celled organisms that eventually led to mammals and thus to us humans.

9   The Anthropic Principle

It can be argued that the biological manifestation of life (biogenesis) as we know it could have only evolved under certain very narrowly defined physical, chemical and astronomical conditions applicable to our universe in general and to our solar system in particular (Matthews, 2005; Reeves, 2005; Fleury, 2006; Reville, 2006; Bogdanov and Bogdanov, 2010; Trinh Xuan Thuan, 2011). In other words, many complex laws of physics operated within *extremely narrow parameters* in order to produce and sustain our universe with its complex living matter. Even *minute* deviations in any one of these cosmic "Fundamental

Constants" (e.g. gravity, the speed of light, the electro-magnetic field, Einstein's cosmic constant, etc.) would have spelt disaster in the tentative and delicate evolution of our universe as a "home" to evolving life (Bogdanov and Bogdanov, 2010). The various physical conditions affecting the Earth (e.g. temperature, acidity, gravity, electromagnetic field, electrostatic force, the position of the Moon relative to the Earth to prevent its wobble, etc.) had to be so precise that one is left wondering if their co-existence could be "merely co-incidental". Even the relationship between these physical conditions (e.g. the ratio of the force of gravity to the force of electromagnetism), if slightly different, would lead to stars either burning out too quickly or to burn too dimly, so that in neither case life as we know it could be supported. If the speed of light were a little faster, oxygen could not have formed, and had the speed of light been a little slower carbon could not have formed. Both oxygen and carbon are essential to life on Earth. If gravity had been stronger the universe would have imploded, and if it had been weaker, galaxies could not have formed. In any case, had the speed of light been different then, stars could not have formed and without stars life on Earth could not have developed (Trinh Xuan Thuan, 2011).

Without the Earth's electro-magnetic field, solar wind radiation would destroy life on Earth. The Earth's electro-magnetic field is created by its outer core of molten iron which behaves like a dynamo. However, if the Earth's inner core were not composed of solid iron then the Earth would wobble, thus rendering it more hostile to the evolution of life as we know it. Without volcanoes we would not have the necessary atmospheric conditions to support life. Volcanic eruptions pumped carbon dioxide into the air, thereby heating it up. This carbon dioxide could be used by plants in photosynthesis to produce oxygen, which in turn could be used by animals in respiration. On the other hand, if there were too many volcanoes, as on Venus for example, then our planet Earth would produce too much carbon dioxide, thereby creating a greenhouse effect and become much too hot to sustain advanced forms of life. Moreover, if the atmospheric pressure were much higher, again as on Venus, then life as we know it could not survive on Earth. If the Earth were closer to the Sun, its water would evaporate and if the Earth were further from the Sun, its water would freeze. Liquid water is essential to advanced forms of life on Earth. The Earth is the right size to hold onto its atmosphere by the force of its gravity. If the orbit of the Earth around the Sun were not stable, then the huge fluctuations of terrestrial temperature would not sustain life on Earth as we know it (Reeves, 2005).The Sun also appears to be burning up at the optimal speed to support life on Earth. If the Sun were combusting more rapidly the Earth would be too hot for life as we know it, and if it were burning up more slowly the Earth could be too cold.

The observation that our universe in general, and the Earth in particular, appear to be so well suited and so finely tuned to support the emergence and sustenance of life has been called the "anthropic principle" (Barrow and Tipler, 1988; Matthews, 2005). It can be argued that the likelihood of all of these pre-requisites coming together simply "by chance" and then going on to produce life "blindly" on Earth, is statistically highly improbable (Bogdanov and Bog-danov, 2010). One would have to postulate that our "special" universe is only one out of millions (if not billions) of other universes, so that *by statistical chance all* of the above criteria for the emergence of human life were met ac-cidentally by our universe! This takes us into the realm of huge metaphysical speculation, as in statistical terms such a probability is close to zero – unless one speculates the existence of an infinite number of universes! How could one demonstrate this scientifically?

Then there is the question of the origin of the "Fundamental Constants" of physics. What determined the speed of light? If these constants arose by chance, one would have to postulate the existence of billions of universes all with different Fundamental Constants and that our universe somehow by chance came up with the correct (for us) combination of constants. This is just more unsupported speculation, sometimes referred to as the "Multiverse Theory", i.e. the theory that there may be billions of universes and that ours by chance is the lucky one!

However, it may also be the case that the Earth's manifestations of life repre-sent just one limited range of environmental adaptations out of a much wider potential spectrum, which may exist elsewhere in our, or in other, universes – as exemplified by the "extremophiles", small living organisms which exist on Earth in very inhospitable environments such as very deep below the Earth's surface, in boiling, acidic or super-saline water or in anoxic (oxygen-free) con-ditions which would kill higher forms of life. This suggests that other (simple?) forms of life could have evolved elsewhere in the universe in extreme condi-tions, perhaps not too dissimilar to those found in the early very inhospitable environments of our young Earth – such as in hydro-thermal vents deep under the sea. However, higher forms of life as we know them would probably not be able to tolerate such extreme conditions.

10   The Evolution of Proteins and of Higher Forms of Life

If the origin of life on Earth was not problematic enough, how about the evo-lution of very basic life forms into more sophisticated forms with their com-plex molecules and metabolisms? There are twenty amino acids in total. They are complex molecules which form the "alphabet" from which proteins are formed. Proteins are composed of long strings of amino acids. Proteins are the building blocks of organisms and are involved in the metabolism (functioning) of all forms of life. Using computer analysis, Wagner (2014) was able to demonstrate that a hypothetical protein "library" of all possible combinations from these 20 amino acids would contain more "volumes" of possible proteins than there are atoms in our universe! It would take billions of years longer than the existence of our universe to come up with a particular desired protein in an organism solely by chance. In other words, random change in DNA (genetic mutations) cannot alone explain evolution by natural selection as there has not been anything near enough time. Luckily, synonymous (similar) "texts" of amino acid sequences can sometimes code for proteins which perform a similar function, e.g. coding for red hair. In other words, there appears to be some built-in redundancy, in that more than one type of protein can code for a trait such as red hair. Nevertheless, Wagner's finding does very seriously question the randomness of evolution given the time scale required.

An even bigger problem exists for metabolism, which involves the interaction of numerous proteins. There are many complex metabolic pathways which would be disrupted if there were even minor changes in amino acid sequences. Luckily there are also some synonymous texts here as well, but the problem remains that there are billions of possible metabolic pathways from which to choose. Random selection cannot readily account for a particular metabolic pathway being "chosen" (e.g. as found in photosynthesis or in respiration via the Krebs Cycle) as our universe in general, and life on Earth in particular is too young at about 3.6 billion years. There simply has not been enough time since life appeared on Earth for randomness to generate the protein and metabolic complexities that we see today, unless there was massive built-in redundancy.

As we mentioned, the same phenotype (such as red hair) can be coded for by more than one genotype. Thus this redundancy slightly alleviates the problem of randomness. Likewise, a given genotype may be able to code for several different phenotypes. If one thinks of genotypes as members of an orchestra, then different circuits of genes (musicians) can play different tunes by playing in different combinations. This is a more dynamic understanding of the functioning of genotypes, which may also partially alleviate the persistent problem of randomness. But what is behind this dynamic?

If the origin of life and of proteins were not problematic enough, how does Darwinian Theory account for the origin of RNA, DNA, genes, meiosis, cells, sexuality, photosynthesis, metamorphosis and, ultimately, for consciousness? For example, cells are chemically very complex. All multi-cellular organisms are formed from similar eukaryotic (nucleus-containing) cells. It is speculated that eukaryotic cells arose just once by chance about 1.4 billion years ago by the fusion of two more primitive (pre-nuclear) prokaryotic cells such as bacteria, archaea or viruses. All higher forms of life thus depend on this supposed once-off accidental fusion. But how and why did lifeless chemicals assemble themselves "spontaneously" into highly organised and functional living units – capable of sexual behaviour and of the very complex chain of chemical reactions required for photosynthesis, etc? Without photosynthesis there would be no oxygen on Earth and without oxygen we could not exist. Moreover, how can non-conscious organic matter become conscious? From where did consciousness come or how was it actually "manufactured" by natural selection? Darwinian Theory can indeed help explain selective forces operating on existing life (e.g. darker skin-types near the equator), but cannot readily account for the emergence of life itself, nor for genes or consciousness. Some of the answers to the above questions may be found in Quantum Biology, so it is to this that we now turn.

11   Quantum Biology

The relatively recent emergence of a counter-intuitive branch of sub-atomic physics applied to biology, namely that of "quantum biology" or also known as "bio-quantum physics", may help unravel some of the above issues. It has been postulated that the physical properties of quantum mechanics can play a role in many biological processes such as bird migration, smell, metamorphosis, photosynthesis, chlorophyll and genetic mutations, to name but a few (Al-Khalili and McFadden, 2014; Al-Khalili, 2017). With "quantum entanglement", related sub-atomic particles such as electrons, protons and photons can "communicate" with each other instantaneously, in other words, faster than the speed of light! A bird, the European robin, can use this property in migration when navigating in the context of the Earth's electro-magnetic field. With the phenomenon called "quantum tunnelling", sub-atomic particles such as protons can pass through barriers, thereby greatly reducing the amount of energy required and thus speeding up bio-chemical reactions, for example as found in enzyme reactions.

"Quantum super-position" implies that sub-atomic particles can have more than one shape and move in many directions simultaneously. This is an aspect of Heisenberg's "uncertainty principle", which states that we cannot know both the momentum and the location of a sub-atomic particle simultaneously. As protons can move simultaneously in many directions, this phenomenon greatly speeds up bio-chemical reactions in a wide range of potential pathways.

Tunnelling and super-position have been implicated in tadpole metamorphosis. The enzymes involved greatly speed up the metabolism associated with metamorphosis, in that their atomic bonds are sensitive to quantum effects. This is also true for the complex metabolisms of photosynthesis and genetic mutations (Al-Khalili and McFadden, 2014).

What we are learning from this new field of quantum physics is that many complex metabolic processes can be enabled and greatly speeded up so that distances, barriers, directions and shapes are no longer the obstacles that we thought they were, when viewed through the lens of classical physics. However, much still remains to be discovered. For example, does quantum biology play a role in consciousness? We know that conscious human observation changes the experimental outcome at the quantum level when trying to detect the position of particles or waves (Al-Khalili and McFadden, 2014). So mind is somehow implicated. The renowned Oxford physicist Sir Roger Penrose postulated that consciousness has quantum origins. Together with Stuart Hameroff, he formulated the "Orchestrated Objective Reduction Theory" of mind which locates consciousness in the microtubules of the brain (Penrose and Hameroff, 2011). Penrose argues that the phenomenon of consciousness cannot be reduced to the type of computations that one finds in computers. For Penrose much of our "computing" occurs at an unconscious level. Here one would tend to agree. Quantum effects may indeed play a role in, or be an aspect of the functioning of consciousness, but to claim that mind can be completely reduced to the principles of quantum biology may be just another reductionist approach. Nevertheless, this is a rapidly developing area of science and new surprises could well be in store!

12   From Rocks to Musicians, Engineers and Philosophers: the Problem of Entropy

Entropy describes the degree of disorder or uncertainty in a system. The Second Law of Thermodynamics states that closed systems will naturally tend towards increased disorder, chaos and randomness. Thus, surprisingly, evolutionary complexification over time operates *against* entropy, i.e. against the general tendency towards *disorder*. Organisms are described as "open systems" which can use an external source of energy (e.g. solar or chemical energy) to decrease their own entropy or disorder.

For many neuro-biologists, what we experience as "mind" is the innocent by-product of the brain in action – which in turn was produced fortuitously *against* the forces of entropy, i.e. against the general tendency towards breakdown, death and decay (what Freud called *Thanatos*, the death instinct). Mind is seen by many scientists as only a secondary epi-phenomenon, spontaneously emergent out of evolving biological matter as expressed by our operative brains (Pinker, 1994, 1997, 2002). So with this view, life (*Eros*) arose casually as a purely chemical and biological phenomenon and subsequently, mind somehow arose out of complex biological matter in just as mysterious a manner as life itself previously came from inanimate inorganic matter. This is a "bottom up" explanation of the emergence of consciousness.

We can thus summarise the dominant view on the origins of life as follows: despite the force of entropy, inorganic matter became more complex via nuclear fusion and somehow evolved into simple *living* matter (vitalisation) capable of self-reproduction (sexual behaviour). So genes somehow assembled themselves, leading to the genetic material of one organism somehow beginning to undergo the complex processes of meiosis and recombination to prepare sperm and ova for fusion with the gametes of another organism. Simple living matter somehow evolved into more complex forms, including those with *consciousness* (mentalisation), culminating in humans capable of using language, playing music, engaging in self-reflection, inquiring into meaning, philosophising and increasingly exercising control over biological evolution via genetic engineering. But why has all this been unfolding and why does evolution, i.e. change, appear to move mainly in one direction, namely that of increased complexity and not also "backwards" towards increased simplicity (given that some simple forms of life such as bacteria are highly fecund, i.e. "successful", in the Darwinian sense)? Is there a problem with this "Mind emergent from Matter" model?

13   The Primacy of Mind over Matter?

Some authors, especially Pierre Teilhard de Chardin (1959), and Sri Aurobindo (1973) and, in his own way, Carl Jung (1958), have envisaged the above relationship the other way around; namely, that "universal mind" or "unmanifest mind" (akin to the "collective unconscious" à la Jung) exists independently of matter and is transcendent. For Teilhard de Chardin, *a priori* or primal consciousness shapes evolution, insofar as the evolutionary process and the resultant biological diversity and sophistication reflect and emanate from "universal mind", meaning that life evolved in its context (Teilhard de Chardin, 1965). From this perspective, unmanifest, universal or "transcendental" mind is part of a greater metaphysical Reality. This Reality expresses itself in the evolution of life by becoming manifest to varying degrees of awareness in embodied consciousness, that is, in "personal mind". The latter in humans, with its individual conscious-ness, is also referred to as the "psyche". This is another way of saying that matter is "bathed" in universal (or transpersonal) mind – rather than mind being sole-ly confined to living (brain) matter. This "top-down" or "collective to personal" understanding of the existence of consciousness is consistent with Jungian psychology, and with the cosmic causality of the ancient Greeks. The latter's theories postulate a form of divine design or permanent structure to the Cos-mos, which should not be confused with contemporary Biblical Creationism, which is largely based on a literal reading of the Book of Genesis. However, the ancient Greek and the Old Testament writers may well have influenced each other as the Hellenistic culture had spread to pre-Christian Israel.

Sheldrake (1988) with his "extended mind" hypothesis offers a similar view to that of transpersonal mind. He postulates the existence of "morphic fields" around the brain, i.e., mind beyond the brain, as well as mind between brains. He explains the latter phenomenon by means of quantum physics by using the analogy of the continuing quantum "entanglement" of systemically related sub-atomic particles even after they have been separated in space. Sheldrake also believes that "memory is inherent in nature" with "morphogenetic" (form giving) fields underlying both energy and matter (Sheldrake, 1988). Such fields therefore act like "blueprints" in the expression of matter – including biologi-cal matter.

Another way of expressing the above is to consider "non-local conscious-ness" as an important part of our non-physical environment. Evidence sug-gests that some aspects of our consciousness transcend the natural boundary of our physical bodies and of our normal sensory mechanisms. Examples of non-local consciousness may include inexplicably accurate hunches, pre-monitions, precognitive dreams and near-death experiences (NDEs). Van Lommel (2010) uses the concept "non-local" consciousness in this context, which is an extension from quantum physics of the construct "quantum non-locality", to explain the influence between objects separated in space – often at great distances.

Just as radios and televisions do not actually create words, music and imag-es, but rather, when tuned into, can capture and relay them, likewise organisms may differ neurologically in their ability to tune into the "mental sea" in which they are bathed. Structural and neurological differences between organisms will reflect their level of ability to access and relay (express) aspects of this transpersonal or "universal mind". This suggests that organisms along the great evolutionary chain of being will manifest different levels of consciousness. In humans, this includes the ability to experience love, compassion and empa-thy, create art, compose classical music, derive mathematical formulae and fathom philosophical concepts such as eternity and infinity. Bio-neurological evolution from this perspective would thus be characterised by increases in attunement with both the physical environment and the "mental sea" (largely unconscious) in which life is evolving. With this model, humans are seen to excel in this attunement to, and personalisation of, "non-local mind" compared with simpler life-forms. Once we humans evolved the prerequisite neurological structures, we were able to "tune into" the truths of mathematics, physics, chemistry, music and so forth.

With the above view, "non-local consciousness" is seen as an essential feature of our non-physical environment. Adaptation to this mental environment via the evolution of personal consciousness would be advantageous. Developing the neurological sophistication to do so would thus be beneficial. Hence, the wide range of psycho-neurological complexities in species that we witness today could be explained, in part, as an evolutionary adaptation to the unmanifest mental environment, by gradually rendering it more conscious. Whereas simpler forms of life are primarily adapted to their physical niches, social animals in general, and humans in particular, also show evidence of adaptation to the postulated "mental sea", with its social and (for humans) aesthetic and spiritual domains. Moreover, our sophisticated sense of aesthetics, humour and morality sets us apart from other forms of life but we may not be the only beings in our universe to have achieved this!

14   From Matter to Culture: a Co-Operative Journey?

But can mind really produce or shape matter? On the other hand, when we look at life solely through the lenses of mainstream evolutionary theory then diverse cultural phenomena such as music, painting, philosophy, poetry, literature, mathematics, architecture and much more, are just envisaged as by-products of the complex workings of human brains which, as already mentioned, purportedly developed via "blind evolution" (Dawkins, 1976). Put differently, human life and all its cultural manifestations are an "accident" of bio-chemical evolution and have no *a priori* meaning *per se*. With this radical materialist model there is an implied primacy of matter over mind, i.e. mind is matter-made – with our "man-made" mind being its ultimate expression – not penultimate to any transpersonal reality. Moreover, from Dawkins's neo-Darwinian perspective, spiritual values are just social meme-correlates, and like all other cultural memes, are purely functional, and are thus devoid of any intrinsic value as such (Hogan, 2008; Weber, 2016).

Theories of biological evolution are based on the environmental selection of the fittest genes. Such selection is not seen to be influenced by any ulterior purpose beyond utility. Dawkins's (1976) view of the "selfish gene" popularised this approach. Genes survive only for the sake of their survival – via sexual and natural selection. Organisms are just vehicles used by genes for the propagation of "selfish" genes. But why do "selfish" genes "need" or "want" to survive? Moreover, it is not just individual genes but whole genotypes, or rather phenotypes (i.e. complex organisms), which are selected or perish. Fitness at the level of a family or group (social cohesion) can also be subjected to selective pressure (O'Connor et al., 2000). So, can all of nature's' wonderful diversity and all of human cultural expression really be reduced to genetic utility and economy? This is unlikely (DelMonte, 2001a, 2005). Weber (2016) also argues strongly against seeing the beauty of nature and of the arts solely in terms of genetic efficiency and functionality. He postulates that there is an excess and surplus of life forms and cultural expression which cannot be simply reduced to economy, usefulness and functionality,

The behaviour of a complex system cannot be explained by only analysing its parts, and certainly not by reducing one's focus to just one component such as genes. When a system reaches a new point of complexity via evolution, unpredicted novel behaviours appear to emerge spontaneously which are greater in sophistication than that shown heretofore by the sum of its parts (DelMonte, 1996; Browne, 2013). It has been postulated that rather than "selfish genes" using bodies to reproduce themselves, it is much more likely to be the other way around: Organisms use their genes to survive and to evolve (Noble, 2006). Noble argues that the weight of evidence in the physiological sciences is now much more favourable to the metaphor of 'co-operation' than of 'selfishness'. "The genes-eye (gene-centric) view is only one way of seeing biology and it doesn't accurately reflect much of what modern biology has revealed" (Noble, 2011, p. 1014).

The evolved complexity and sophistication of animal and human behaviour (including altruism, respect, compassion and affection), the sophistication of the world's cultural achievements and the profound archetypal symbolisation associated with the major religions, wisdom-traditions and philosophies of the world, is breathtaking. It is surely very parsimonious indeed to put all of this down to some unprompted evolutionary by-product of "selfish genes", as the advocates of neo-Darwinian biological primacy would postulate.

Although aggressive competition between organisms and "survival of the fittest" is a feature of evolution, co-operation between organisms and symbiosis are overall much more common phenomena. For example, algae were greatly helped in colonising land from the ancient seas in which they evolved by forming symbiotic relationships with fungi. Algae had no roots but fungi could provide the anchorage, minerals, carbon dioxide and water needed by the algae. In return, the algae provided carbohydrates for the fungi. All of this allowed the simple algae to evolve into the higher plants so essential to animal life. These higher plants continue to form similar symbiotic relationships with fungi in their roots.

Besides the numerous examples of intra-species and inter-species co-operation and of various symbiotic relationships involving animals and plants, we humans host a vast range of bacteria in our intestines and we have co-evolved with them to our mutual benefit. This phenomenon is sometimes re-ferred to as "sym-biogenesis" (Noble, 2011; Browne, 2013). Lamarck in the 18th century had already noted such co-operation between species, as did Darwin later on.

15   The Animal Mind—Ethology

Even at the animal level (especially with social insects, birds and mammals) the detailed intricacies of social behaviour are often suspiciously more com-plex and purposeful than can be comfortably accounted for by random (mostly deleterious) mutations, natural selection, genetic founder effects and genetic drift. The existence of metamorphosis and of very complex polymorphous life cycles (sometimes linked to very long distance migrations, as with the monarch butterfly), as well as of behaviours such as variable camouflage (by some fish and octopuses), mimicry, deception, inter-species exploitation, inter-species partnership, intra-species nurturing, inter-species playfulness, complex court-ing and mating rituals, hunting pack team-work and the like, all point to so-phisticated, highly developed levels of social organisation in animals requiring some level of consciousness. There appears to be a missing factor in many me-chanical explanations of animal behaviour. Some rather spectacular examples will help to illustrate this point.

How did some birds learn to eat morsels of food from the teeth of croc-odiles while standing in their open mouths? How did monkeys who eat poisonous leaves learn to eat certain clays and charcoal as antidotes? More spectacularly, how did monkeys learn to use insect-repellent tree sap and to bite poisonous insects in order to provoke them to release poisonous toxins for rubbing into their fur to kill off parasites? How did some snakes, spiders and scorpions develop the complex concoctions involved in the manufacture of poisons such as haemotoxins, cytotoxins and neurotoxins without harm-ing themselves? How did "forest witch" plants "learn" to lure and trap insects inside their slippery receptacles, which two days later become less slippery, thus allowing the insects to crawl out covered in pollen, thereby enabling the pollination of other plants? What does one think about a small crustacean that invades a larger crustacean, castrates it and in so doing turns it into a "maternal factory" for its own progeny?! Then there is a worm that invades the brain of frogs, thereby slowing them down and making it easier to be caught and eaten by herons, which subsequently spread the worm's eggs in their droppings. There is also a fungus which infects the brain of ants which then crawl to the top of grass blades at the right time of day to be eaten by herbivores. There is the remarkable case of a toxoplasma parasite that, by infecting the brain of mice, fatally renders them attracted to the smell of cats and their urine. Having eaten such an infected mouse the cat then spreads the parasite in its faeces. Finally, but not exhaustively, how did birds learn to bring insecticidal plants into their insect-infested nests full of chicks? Could not the evolving use of some type of consciousness rather than "blind evolution" play the decisive role here?

The utilisation by animals of plants, fungi and certain clay minerals to improve their health, fight disease, ward off parasitic infestations and achieve drug-induced altered states of consciousness is quite remarkable. So are the various manifestations of primitive culture and of social co-operation among animals such as a sense of unfairness, empathy, etc., as found in certain monkeys and apes (Lestel, 2003; de Waal, 2006, 2013). Self-awareness, previously thought to be a uniquely human feature, has now also been demonstrated in chimpanzees, elephants and dolphins (Lestel, 2003; de Waal, 2006, 2013; Ameisen, 2012). Crows, chimps and bonobos are also capable of deceitful behaviour, thereby fooling their competitors, showing that they have developed an understanding that we all do not necessarily share the same perspective. Lying or deceiving successfully (e.g. by some birds and snakes "playing dead") may require a level of self-awareness which allows an animal to know that what goes on in the mind of others may be different from what his own mind knows. This "mind reading" ability to understand the mental state of oneself and others has been called "Theory of Mind" (Fonagy, 2011), but heretofore it has largely been seen as a human trait. Reeves (2005, 2011) argues strongly for a continuity between pre-human and human life.

Regarding the behaviour of non-human life, we know that both animals and plants evolved to be sensitive to the influence of the sun and the moon. Plants orientate towards sunlight and open or close their pores accordingly. The reproductive, feeding and migratory behaviour of many animals is strongly influenced by solar and lunar factors. They are subject to the same fundamental laws that govern us humans, including those of quantum biology. Many species appear to demonstrate simple consciousness, and, as already mentioned, a few species appear to be capable of some degree self-consciousness or reflection. Thus can the beauty found in living organisms be simply reduced to its 'usefulness', or does it express a higher order aesthetic sense as is argued by Weber (2016)? Is this gradual acquisition of all aspects of consciousness a universal evolutionary process? It may be so. Take for example the species of wood-ants. They usually live in large colonies whose members are genetically very closely related. When members of one colony meet members of other colonies they typically fight to the death. Yet somehow there more recently evolved some super-colonies of wood-ants of mixed genetic background whose members live in co-operative harmony together. This example illustrates a direction of evolution from very local survival to co-operation on a larger scale. In summary, there evolved three types or "levels" of co-operation: Firstly, as found at the level of the family as in parenting. The next level is within species as in ant colonies, flocks of birds, shoals of fish, herds of mammals and so forth. At a higher level one finds inter-species symbiosis, co-operation and even apparent altruism as illustrated above. Although we have focussed on the animal kingdom, it has also been argued that plants, especially mature trees, show a capacity for communication and inter-connectedness. Peter Wohlleben referred to this phenomenon as a "wood wide web" (Wohlleben, 2016).

16   The Missing Ingredient: Mind?

Can Darwinian selection really account for *all* of this complexity in life? Parsimony does not guarantee accuracy! Simply throwing in the "solution" of the passage of time does not solve the dilemma of the statistical improbability of all of this complexity occurring solely at random. Who really believes that if monkeys had typewriters and interminable time, they would ever accidentally produce anything resembling the works of Shakespeare, Jane Austen, Proust, Dante or Goethe? Moreover, why should they even bother trying, given that such exhaustive and complex productions are unlikely to yield more substantial sexual selective advantage than, say, brute force? Rape may make reproductive (selfish gene) sense but may not yield ethical peace of mind. Why should this matter so much, if we are no more than elaborate non-moral vehicles surrounding "selfish-genes"? Can it really be argued that artistic ability only evolved because it offers a selective advantage, i.e. more offspring? Why does artistic symbolisation, allowing us to understand one sign as representing another object or idea, exist so extensively in humans? More to the point, given that many, if not most, lower forms of life such as bacteria and ants have high selective (i.e. reproductive) fitness, why should humans have evolved at all? Ants with their tiny brains nevertheless evolved complex social structures and communicate via sounds, postures, "dances" and chemically. They are so successful that they account for about ten percent of the total animal biomass of the world (Passera, 2006). Ants can use disease-infected ants to immunise other ants in the colony against a particular infection. They are also capable of forming symbiotic relationships with aphids, in which the ants provide protection for the aphids, in return for some of the sugar which the latter produce. Some birds, e.g. the east African honey-guide bird, are known to lead members of the Boran People to honey which they then share. These "indicator" birds use a song specific to this relationship with the Boran honey gatherers. In the same vein, bottlenose dolphins in Brazil help fishermen catch fish by driving them shore-wards, which they then share in a win-win situation. Complex, interdependent awareness is involved in these examples.

With the current trend towards bio-medical materialism, with its over-reliance on bio-technology and pharmacotherapy, one is at risk of losing sight of the intentional and spiritual aspects of what it is to be alive and human. It would appear that the neo-Darwinian view of evolution as well as those hypotheses which focus primarily on the biological domain (e.g. on the radical materialism of social Darwinism and socio-biology), although interesting, are in their own particular ways simplifying the enormous complexities involved. At best they are only partial explanations. An example of such a partial explanation is the newly emerging discourse of "evolutionary psychiatry" which attempts to explain most psychiatric disorders primarily from the perspective of Darwinian Theory (Stevens and Price, 1996).

17   Are There Limits to Darwinian Theory?

Darwin was puzzled by the rapid appearance and spread of flowering plants (angiosperms) and in 1879 famously referred to this as an "abominable mystery". Darwin's theory of natural selection was predicated on slow, gradual changes over long periods of time, in which all intermediate steps in the evolutionary process of an organism had to have survival value. Naturally-occurring mutations of genes and recombination meiosis produced the genetic variability upon which selection was based (Darlington, 1966; Carter, 1970). Yet this does not explain at a deeper level the quantity and quality of the potential variation upon which selection operates. Moreover, the fossil evidence does not always support the view that evolution was gradual. In the past, periods of very slow evolution in life-forms, not far from equilibrium, have been punctu-ated by periods of very rapid evolutionary change. This phenomenon is called "punctuated equilibria" (Gould, 1977, 2002).

Cosmic radiation, background radiation from the earth, naturally-occurring chemical mutagens and copying errors in meiosis have been assumed to be responsible for these genetic mutations – but there is no compelling evidence that all mutations to genes can be accounted for in this way (Carter, 1970). Moreover, it is not just genes that mutate. Chromosomes too can undergo drastic changes – namely translocations and breakages resulting in chromo-somal insertions, deletions, inversions, etc. There are also chromosomal non-disjunctions resulting in trisomy (an additional chromosome) and monosomy (a missing chromosome), etc. (Carter, 1970). Such macro-level changes to the genotype may have "revolutionary" consequences, leading to evolutionary "leaps" if successful. These large chromosomal changes can be contrasted with micro-level changes associated with genetic mutations and recombination meiosis, in that their consequences were often much more dramatic. Moreo-ver, genetic information is not only passed downwards to the next generation, but also transposed horizontally within and between many species – especial-ly with respect to retro-viruses, bacteria and plants (McClintock, 1961).

The question is, are all mutations to genes and to chromosomes, as well as meiosis, really entirely random? Could there be a larger background or "field", as well as the laws of physics and chemistry, in the context of which mutations take place and to which genetic mutations are subjected, there-by imposing structure and direction to evolution? What really constitutes the environment in which selection takes place? At a micro-level, does it in-clude the properties of the atomic nucleus? Al-Khalili and McFadden (2014) produced evidence that quantum biology may play a role in mutations. At a macro-level it certainly includes our proximate physical environment, other organisms, climatic conditions and our distal environment (the sun, moon, etc). How do we know that it does not include more, yet to be ascertained – or unascertainable – factors (such as "dark matter", "dark energy" or something akin to consciousness or "universal mind")? Sun-spots, electro-magnetic and gravitational fields are other examples of timeless physical forces which may influence and shape events. Mathematical laws (geometric laws, pi, fractals, integers, prime numbers, irrational numbers, etc) are likewise transcendent to the human condition – as mathematical truths exist both before and after our lifetimes and are not dependent on us for their verity. Is there, thus, a sub-text, "para-text" or "supra-text" which guides evolution, giving it direction and defining the parameters of its range of expression? The laws of physics, chem-istry and mathematics have governed the evolution of our universe ever since the hypothetical "Big Bang" (and maybe existed prior to it), so how could the evolution of life escape their, and perhaps other, prescriptions? Since all matter is composed of atoms, could it be that atoms contain information necessary to evolution?

Recent evidence suggests that the evolution of complex new forms of life, rather than requiring many new genes or genetic mutations, can be accomplished by relatively small adjustments to existing genes, involving relatively few changes to the DNA sequences (Yoon, 2007). In other words, new species do not necessarily require new genes, but rather modifications to the expression of existing ones, as for example appears to be the case with humans and chimpanzees, who, depending on whether or not one includes genetic insertions and deletions, share between 96 and 99 percent of their genetic material. The developmental expression of genes is influenced systemically by master and control genes, which in turn are influenced by environmental, neuronal, hormonal and psychological factors. This is called epi-genetics. A good example of this is the fact that even though all the cells of a given organism contain the same genotype, the cells of its bodily organs are phenotypically different. Brain cells do not look like heart, muscle or kidney cells.

More interestingly, genetic material appears to be anticipatory, for example, fish appear to possess the genetic potential for making fingers, hands and feet – as if preparing for land usage (Yoon, 2007). In other words, major evolutionary transitions and advances were not necessarily triggered by genetic mutations so as to code for the new body-parts. In fact most mutations, i.e. changes at the level of DNA, do not have a measurable phenotypic effect under normal physiological conditions (Noble, 2011). Instead the right environmental conditions may have set new developmental structures in motion, via the selective expression of already existing genetic potential under the control of master genes. Hence the total environment is implicated – from a mother's emotional attunement to possible cosmic realities beyond our ken. The former, mother's attunement, affects ontogeny, and the latter, cosmic reality, may guide phylogeny via natural laws and, perhaps, via what has metaphysically been referred to as "universal" or "non-local" mind – a global field. Could the latter be an over-arching aspect of all laws?

18   Wallace's Perspective: Teleological Considerations

Alfred Russel Wallace (1823–1913), Charles Darwin's contemporary, but largely overlooked, was a co-proponent of evolution by natural selection. He believed in some kind of "Higher Intelligence" guiding the more important aspects of

evolution – such as the origin of life on Earth, the emergence of consciousness and the development of civilisation. These changes implied major steps
forward in spirituality for Wallace (1870). Wallace was an enthusiastic field stu-
dent of evolution. He was a pioneer in "mouth-gesture theory", that is the view
that the expressiveness of speech as seen in the mouth by tooth, lip and tongue
movement and in breathing, is a factor in the origin of language communication. For instance, the mouth closes at the end of the sound "come" (indicating
movement towards the speaker) and opens at the end of "go", indicating de-
parture. These contrastive pairings are found in a number of languages (Wallace, 1895).Wallace was thus also a pioneer in bio-semiotics, i.e. the study of
biological signs as a form of communication. His contemporary, the American
pragmatic philosopher Charles Sanders Peirce (1839–1914), was a co-pioneer in
bio-semiotics. Both Wallace and Peirce argued that our bodily gestures are not
just physical phenomena, as they also convey social and emotional meaning.

Wallace noted that natural selection operates without the benefit of pre-
adaptational foresight. Wallace, unlike Darwin and also unlike Lamarck half
a century earlier, did not believe in the inheritance of acquired characteristics
or Lamarckism. Darwin accepted Lamarck's view that characteristics acquired
during an organism's lifetime could be passed on to its progeny. (Neither Darwin nor Wallace would have been aware of genetics and thus of epi-genetic
effects or of mitochondrial inheritance). So, if there is no (genetic) inheritance
of acquired characteristics and no pre-adaptational foresight in natural selection, then how come we human beings have reached such an advanced level
of sophistication in cultural matters? Wallace contended that many human
features are largely inexplicable by natural selection, e.g. speech, singing, artistic notions (of form, texture and colour), mathematical and geometrical reasoning, morality, ethical values and concepts such as eternity and infinity. The
latter attributes, as well as our multiform cultural expressions, are far more
complex than required in order to survive the crude forces of natural selection (DelMonte, 2001a, 2005). There thus appears to be a striking surplus of
knowledge – and of aesthetic expression! (Damasio, 2018). Weber (2016) also
postulates that this surplus, excess and diversity of aesthetics in nature and in
human cultural activity cannot be reduced to the operation of selfish genes as
Dawkins has argued. We, like bacteria, can produce plenty of healthy offspring
(reproductive fitness) without any of these higher capacities. Wallace envisaged a form of teleological natural selection in which everything that exists
in life has a purpose – be it utilitarian (e.g. long necks), aesthetic or spiritual.

Wallace noted the problem of incipient (intermediate) evolutionary stages.
He argued that incipient stages may have little selective survival advantage,
e.g., partially developed wings or eyes, or a part of the complex chemical chain

of reactions required in photosynthesis or in metamorphosis. Yet evolution progressed in complexity as if teleologically guided. Wallace thus predicted the problem of "irreducible complexity": he noted that if only one part of a complex whole is missing then it can no longer function, e.g., as with biological "clocks" (Behe, 2004). A group composed of paleo-anthropologists and paleo-linguists also argued that both the physical and cognitive articulations required for human speech are so sophisticated that it is difficult to imagine intermediary systems (Picq et al., 2008). They described as a neo-Darwinian tautology the argument that if a human feature existed then it must be adaptive otherwise it would not have survived, because this is a form of Panglossian, post-hoc reasoning. How did the complex rules of grammar and syntax evolve? When it comes to semantics, how and why did abstract nouns and concepts such as infinity, zero and eternity evolve? Do they really convey selective advantage and reproductive fitness?

Wallace did not see mind as solely a manifestation of the brain in action. For Wallace "disconnected mind" (or non-local mind) belongs to the spiritual world, where "Higher Intelligence" operates as a guiding force in the development of higher human capacities. Natural selection, whilst accounting for the adaptational progress of biological evolution, has little or nothing to do with the greater "mysteries of life" according to Wallace (1870).

Why has Wallace, the Welsh co-founder of the theory of natural selection with Darwin, been so ignored? Was it because his approach was both aetiological and teleological? Darwin's purely aetiological, rather functional "survival of the fittest" perspective, was much more parsimonious and more compatible with the emerging scientific positivism, materialism, atheism, individualism and competitive free-enterprise views of the West. Darwin's vision was more closely allied to the philosophy of materialism, thus to atheism, and to the view that mind emerged from matter. On the other hand, Wallace's perspective was largely consistent with Greek idealist philosophy and also with spirituality, in that "disconnected" mind was not seen as the product of matter. His perspective has increasingly been over-shadowed by advocates of materialist reductionism.

19   Evolutionary Patterns

One has to accept that, for the time being, teleological considerations are largely metaphysical speculations, although as William Blake said, what is now proved was once only imagined. However, the point which we wish to emphasise is that, just as there are mathematical, geometrical, musical, linguistic, electro-magnetic and gravitational patterns and forms, likewise the forms (or structures) of life emergent from evolution may not be random. They may, in a "big-picture" macro-sense, be reflective of universal laws, such as Einstein's General Theory of Relativity and Field Theory, and in a micro-sense be consistent with sub-particle quantum physics, and thus not solely the outcome of random mutations and natural selection in the strict Darwinian sense. We can clearly observe patterns, e.g. symmetry, in plant and animal life forms. These have been referred to as obeying "laws of biological form" (Davey, 1981). This is, of course, a view which is consistent with Plato's five basic solid shapes (shapes believed to encompass the fundamental components of the physical universe) and with his Theory of Forms, which asserts that all manifest things are reflections of their pre-existing, eternal, changeless Form (Jowett, 1888).

It can be argued that the fundamental laws of mathematics influence the patterning of physical objects and of living organisms. As far back as the 13th century, the Italian mathematician Leonardo Pisano (also known as Fibonacci) discovered what are now known as "Fibonacci numbers" – 1, 2, 3, 5, 8, 13, 21, 34, etc. One simply adds the last two numbers to generate the next one. Fibonacci number patterns are ubiquitous in nature. Plants illustrate the Fibonacci series in the numbers and arrangements of petals, leaves, sections and seeds. It can be found in tree branching, phyllotaxis (the arrangement of leaves on a stem), the uncurling of ferns, fruit sprouts of pineapples, the flowering of artichokes, the arrangement of the pine cone's bracts and the like. These beautiful patterns are also referred to as the Golden Section of Nature. Many scientists saw a link between beauty and truth. This was particularly true for Albert Einstein, Isaac Newton and Paul Dirac. For Dirac, the closer we approach the truths of mathematics and physics, the more beautiful the world appears.

There is thus a discernible interplay between mathematics and biology (Trinh Xuan Thuan, 2011). Another example is the symmetry of the hexagonal pattern found in the honeycombs of bee-hives. This is the most geometrically efficient way to construct a honeycomb. How did bees come up with this pattern, which is also found in non-biological nature, for example as in snowflakes and the volcanic rocks of the Giants' Causeway in the north of Ireland?

Before the Big Bang, there supposedly was just a stable singularity or a "super-symmetry" (Bogdanov and Bogdanov, 2010), i.e. a unity without pattern, space or time, without matter as we know it, i.e. only with coded potential ("unmanifest mind" perhaps?) – rather like a tiny seed ready to unfold, not at random, but rather according to pre-existing laws. As Einstein said, "God does not play at dice with the universe!" From the Big Bang onwards, patterns began to emerge in space and time. Matter took form and increased in complexity, in accordance with the fundamental laws of physics, chemistry and mathematics

(DelMonte, 2005, 2011a; Reeves, 2011). From laboratory observations we know that at a physical level, patterns may appear spontaneously, producing regularities out of microscopic chaos (Capra and Luisi, 2014). Sometimes such patterns are established and maintained (e.g. in crystals) in the absence of any apparent external causation, thus in apparent violation of the Second Law of Thermodynamics which governs entropy. (See Ramseyer and Tschacher, 2006, for a further discussion of the work of Prigogine, Haken, and others).

Moreover, on a much larger scale, curved space-time, electro-magnetic patterns, geometrical and mathematical patterns (e.g., prime numbers, Fibonacci numbers, pi and fractals) and indeed much more, characterise our universe. Life also evolved. It too is patterned. So are languages, human behaviour, music and so forth. Such patterning led the ancient Greek philosopher Socrates to speculate about cosmic intelligent design. So what was there before the Big Bang to trigger it and create all of these forms and patterns? What determined the Laws of Nature? For Bogdanov and Bogdanov (2010) and Reeves (2011) the structure of our universe, life and consciousness were emergent out of universal laws from the moment of the Big Bang and thus were neither directionless nor entirely random. There is only a limited randomness, within parameters, but enough to ensure that not every detail of our existence is entirely predictable (Reeves, 2011).

Classical Darwinian Theory, centred on reproductive fitness (i.e. the number of progeny) does not address the above issues, nor was it intended to do so. Darwin's views, whilst accounting for the details of micro-evolution, such as the prevalence of darker skin in the tropics, do not address the really big questions (Gee, 2000). In other words, Darwinian selection undoubtedly accounts for the detailed "fine-tuning" of biological diversity (micro-evolution), but not so readily for the issues at the level of the grander "scheme of things" (macro-evolution), such as the emergence of living genes, cells, organisms, consciousness and the existence of complex life forms, as well as repetitive patterns such as biological symmetry, social behaviour, reflective consciousness, compassion, non-genetic altruism, morality and aesthetics (e.g. the Golden Mean).

Broad (1925) argued that natural selection is a negative process in that it tends to eliminate individuals who have variations unfavourable to survival. Hence natural selection (elimination) cannot entirely account for production, that is, for the origin and growth in complexity of mind (consciousness). Other authors have also drawn attention to the problem of the origin of conscious cognition (Lindahl, 1997; Arhem and Liljenstrom, 1997). Life and consciousness could not have emerged out of matter if it were not consistent with fundamental universal laws (DelMonte, 2005, 2011a; Reeves, 2011) – regardless of natural selection. In Darwinian Theory, fitness to survive and to reproduce is the ultimate goal. As already pointed out, very primitive organisms do an excellent job here, so materialistically there is no biological imperative for higher forms of life with consciousness to evolve.

In summary, the Darwinian view is too focussed on minute adaptational changes (e.g. the colour of moths) to account for the "bigger picture" of evolution. Evidence for Darwinian Theory is based on additive details of research, i.e. on what George Kelly (1955) called the "accumulative fragmentalism" typical of simple linear causality research – a model which is now increasingly being contested (DelMonte, 1996: Brown, 2013; Capra and Luisi, 2014). Life on Earth is part of a massive complex system or web where causal relationships tend to be intricate, hierarchical and circular. This bigger picture sees life emerging and evolving in the context of our universe itself evolving. The contemporary product which we currently witness, namely reflective, ethical and aesthetic human life, evolved out of organic matter, which itself evolved out of inorganic material. So, is mind really "caused" by matter?

20   Circular Causality: a Systemic Approach

Objections may also be raised to the earlier metaphysical postulations that "universal" (or "non-local") mind somehow "causes" or creates matter, i.e. that matter is mind-made. Another view is that mind and matter co-evolve and are not separate entities, but rather manifestations of the same phenomenon *at different levels of abstraction*. In other words, the dualistic view of linear causality, as in biological determinism, whereby matter "causes" mind (or vice versa), is usefully replaced by the non-dualistic concept of "linguistic parallelism" (Hogan, 1995) in which psyche and soma (i.e. mind and body) are perceived as polymorphic manifestations at different levels of concreteness or abstraction. Here, by way of a crude analogy, we can think, metaphorically, of water molecules existing polymorphically in solid, liquid and gaseous forms. This view is consistent with the 17th century Dutch monist and pantheist philosophy of Baruch de Spinoza, who in his major work "Ethics" (1677) argued that matter and mind are differentiated attributes of one and the same substance – namely that of (non-dual) "Nature/God", and thus there is no need to infer linear causality (Guenancia, 2009). God is nature, and thus nature is not created by God. Similarly, the Dalai Lama stated that "the mind can in no sense be the substantial cause of matter, nor can matter be that of the mind" (Dalai Lama, 2002, p.323). In other words, consciousness does not emerge from the evolution of matter, but rather co-evolved from the beginning together with matter, manifesting initially as simple non-conscious information processing life-forms, and much more recently as conscious, self-reflective humans.

The above views of Spinoza, the Dalai Lama and Hogan are very consistent with Taoists Yin-Yang philosophy and with those of the Greek philosopher Heraclitus, both schools of thought emerging about 500 years BC. Heraclitus postulated a "Harmony of Opposites", i.e. a fundamental unity between apparently opposite phenomena, as, for example with mind and matter.

It is very likely that consciousness, like the fundamental laws of physics, cannot be reduced to any other cause. In this sense it may also be as fundamental as the laws of gravity, space-time, mass, etc. (Chalmers, 2010, 2012). Materialist philosophy cannot explain the emergence of consciousness out of matter. If consciousness is as fundamental as the givens of physics, then it cannot be explained away by matter, as it was co-existent with it from the beginning, albeit in potential, unmanifest or very simple form. This non-explaining away is also true for mass, light and the other fundamentals of our physical universe. It is also contended that consciousness may be "universal", that is, an inherent property of all matter and energy in the universe (Chalmers, 2010, 2012). Here consciousness is seen as analogous to information processing. Higher forms of life such as humans and dolphins would thus have higher consciousness/information processing capacity than bacteria and viruses. Insects would have higher consciousness/information processing ability than plants, which in turn would have more information processing capacity than molecules and atoms. This trend could be reduced right down to sub-atomic particles. Thus when these particles combine to form atoms, and then go on to form molecules, cells, simple organisms and complex forms of life there is, with this panpsychist hypothesis, an increase in information processing ability and thus in consciousness from sub-atomic particle right up to humans. Thus, with the evolution of matter, i.e. the appearance of forms with ever-increased material complexity, consciousness also appears to emerge with this increased complexity.

Simple manifestations of consciousness may thus be akin to basic information processing, as found in all forms of life. Somewhat higher expressions of consciousness may be non-conscious emotions. Here emotion refers to the organisms' unconscious capacity to respond with motion either in terms of its physiology, bio-chemistry or even in terms of behavioural reflexes (Damasio and Carvalho 2013). At a higher level, emotions become conscious as feelings, and at an even higher level as feelings upon which the organism can reflect and decide on a response.

In this context, the notion of simple linear causality, with its attendant model of one-way primary causes, is no longer seen to be useful (Maturana, 1978;

Varela and Maturana, 1981; Capra and Luisi, 2014). Systemic circular "causality", which can also include the concept of an "ultima ratio" (a direction or an ultimate raison d'être), is probably a more useful way to conceive of evolution. With this view, aetiology, the push of the past, is systemically balanced by teleology – the pull of the future. At the time of the Big Bang, i.e. at the dawn of our time, there was, in a sense, only teleology and no aetiology – no past and only future; although with circular "causality", potentiality and teleology cannot be clearly differentiated. Since, from the moment of the Big Bang, the Cosmic Constants (or Fundamental Constants) and other universal laws were already in place, the end product of self-conscious life was (probably) entirely predictable (Bogdanov and Bogdanov, 2010; Reeves, 2011). This is particularly so if the potential for an unfolding consciousness itself is one of the Cosmic Fundamentals. It would also help to explain why various levels of consciousness appear to be so universal throughout the animal kingdom.

Thus, with this view, aetiology and teleology are simply two faces of the same coin. Life as we know it may have been inevitable rather than accidental. Moreover, for a photon (light particle) travelling at the speed of light, from 380,000 years after the Big Bang when light first appeared, up to the present moment there is no passage of time at all (Bogdanov and Bogdanov, 2010). In other words, past and present are confounded when it comes to light particles. It all unfolded at once from the perspective of a photon!

21   The Mind/Brain Issue

The American psychologist William James (1902) was a strong critic of material reductionism when coming to an understanding of consciousness. He coined the term "a stream of consciousness" and advocated the inter-dependence of mind and body. Another aspect of this systemic view is Gregory Bateson's (1972) contention that mind is not just immanent (emergent) from the brain but from the whole body, plus the whole interactive context, including the social environment. This is another way of saying that, paradoxically, mind has both immanent and transcendent aspects. This echoes Wallace's (1870) views on "disconnected mind" and Sheldrake's (1988) on "extended mind", as well as van Lommel's (2010) postulate of "non-local mind". Likewise, some scientists have argued that mind is not just simply confined to the brain and the central nervous system, but is also emergent (subconsciously) from the whole body with its peripheral nervous system (Pert, 1998, 1999; Sthalekar, 2000), e.g. we can "feel" with our hearts and intestines in that they are neurologically and endocrinologically complex, being enriched with neuro-peptide receptors.

Neuro-peptides are produced in neurones (nerve cells) and travel down their long axons, acting throughout the nervous system and beyond into other parts of the body (Browne, 2013). Moreover, the cardiac atrium produces a hormone called "atrial natriuretic factor" (ANF) which interacts with other hormones and thus has an influence over the whole cardiovascular system, affecting all major organs in the body. ANF has an impact on the limbic system of the brain and hence on the thalamus and the pituitary gland. ANF is also involved in the immune system and affects the pineal gland, influencing the production and action of melatonin which plays a role in our sleep patterns (Browne, 2013). When one considers the effect of neuro-peptides and ANF on our bodies, expressions such as "gut feelings", "felt gutted", "no stomach for a fight", "butter-flies in the stomach", "I felt it in my bones", "I had a sixth sense", "heart-felt", "broken hearted", "sweetheart", "big hearted", "warm hearted", "cold hearted" "kind hearted", "soft hearted" "heavy hearted" "light hearted", "half-hearted", etc., begin to make more sense!

A problem with Dawkins's radical "selfish gene" determinism is that his neo-Darwinian model is based on simple linear causality. If we think of life on Earth as a complex inter-dependent living biosphere à la the Gaia Hypothesis (Lovelock, 2000; Capra and Luisi, 2014) then a systemic approach would make more sense. For example, when one notes the high degree of collective co-operation in the social insects (such as bees, ants and termites) and, especially, the speed and manoeuvrability of shoals of fish and flocks of birds, one is left with the impression that they offer us a possible example of what could be called a systemic "group mind" in operation (McDougall, 1921; Sheldrake 1988). This phenomenon has also been referred to as "collective cognition" (Couzin, 2008). In humans it is colloquially, and often pejoratively, referred to as "group hysteria".

22   Genetic Expression: a Systemic View

From a systemic point of view, genes cannot be selfish. Genes within an organism need to co-operate rather than to compete, as they either survive or perish together. Although each cell of a given organism contains exactly the same genotype, the expression of its genes varies hugely depending on whether they are coding for bone tissue, heart muscle, brain cells and so forth. In so doing, the genotype of an organism expresses itself "upwards" as a complex phenotype. But this phenotypic expression also changes over time, depending on the aging process and also on environmental factors.

The whole sentient organism can also act "downwards" from the mind, epi-genetically, to influence a range of co-ordinated gene expressions which can fluctuate – even within hours. This has been called "downward causation" (Noble, 2006, 2011; Capra and Luisi, 2014). For instance, prolonged negative rumination, as found in chronic depression, can depress the immune system, leading to physical illness. Hence genes co-operate systemically, more like a symphony, both within the whole organism but also within individual cells (Noble, 2006, 2011). Seeing the human species as a loosely held together mega-organism adapting to a complex environment in numerous ways, so as to ensure that a wide variety of skills are developed – e.g., maternal empathy, mechanical skills, abstract reasoning – is consistent with a systemic view in which all types of human endeavour are selected for in order to produce an evolving, adaptive, coherent and functioning whole.

23   Evolution: a Systemic Approach

We can recapitulate the arguments thus far: Since the Big Bang, matter has been evolving from sub-atomic particles into atoms, simple molecules, complex inorganic molecules, organic molecules, uni-cellular organisms such as bacteria, eukaryotic cells, organisms, eventually culminating in conscious, reflective and social forms of life. It had been observed for centuries that evolution moves in the direction of increased complexity. Already in the 18th century Jean-Baptiste Lamarck, a French biologist, noted that there was a force driving evolution from simple to complex forms. This hypothesis of a complexifying tendency was further elaborated on by Pierre Teilhard de Chardin in the 20th century. He also postulated that evolution movement in the direction of increasing complexity is allied with a concomitant rise in consciousness. He called this phenomenon the "Law of Complexity-Consciousness" (Teilhard de Chardin, 1965).

The Irish psychiatrist Ivor Browne (2013), in discussing this evolutionary complexification, refers to social animals such as termites, ants, bees, apes and humans as potential "third order living systems": cells being first order and organisms second order living systems. First order systems (cells) can combine and co-operate to produce second order systems (organisms) which have characteristics that are greater than the sum of their (first order) parts – such as increased information processing ability/consciousness. Likewise, second order systems, like individual termites or humans, can function as a third order system when they behave collectively as in termite colonies or as in human families, political groups, etc., again usually displaying higher levels of complexity than found at the second order level. It can also be argued that all life on our planet – the biosphere – is an integrated fourth order system. Lovelock's (2000) Gaia Hypothesis comes to mind here. Is our solar system, with its lunar, solar and wider cosmic influences, a vast fifth order system? We live on a tiny planet in a vast universe, with its cosmic laws and perturbations.

Regarding the universe, the Russian physical chemist Ilya Prigogine was awarded the Nobel Prize in 1977 for his work on the thermodynamics of non-equilibrium systems. Whereas "closed systems" in our universe appear to operate like stable machines, this is not true for "open systems" (e.g. organisms). Closed systems appear to only constitute a small part of the universe. Open systems are characterised by change, instability and continual fluctuation (Browne, 2013; Capra and Luisi, 2014). Prigogine described "self-organising" systems as having special characteristics, such as irreversibility and non-linear transformations under conditions far from stable equilibrium. He extended the properties of the Second Law of Thermodynamics to open systems, to show that new properties could emerge which heretofore did not pertain. These new properties include a capacity for "self-organisation", so that a spontaneous higher level of organisational complexity can emerge (Prigogine and Stengers, 1984, Browne, 2013; Capra and Luisi, 2014). The potential for these emergent higher levels of organisation must have been present in matter from the beginning, otherwise how could they have emerged?

Open systems can locally achieve an increase in structural order, and thus in complexity, by ingesting, processing and assimilating the negative entropy (i.e. orderliness) previously possessed by structures in its surroundings. They then expel back into their environment "waste products" which are at a higher order of positive entropy (i.e., of dis-orderliness) than those which it had previously ingested. Such ingestion of order increases the energy level of the open system, so that it eventually moves further from equilibrium and is thus likely to show an increase in instability, fluctuation and turbulence. This fluctuation can eventually become so powerful that it de-stabilises the pre-existing systemic organisation, until it reaches a "bi-furcation point" of radical change. This initiates the emergence of new unforeseeable organisations ranging from chaos to higher organisation, which are irreversible (Prigogine and Stengers, 1984; Browne 2013). This is what appears to happen in evolution, but mainly, thus overall, in the direction of increased complexity.

Life on Earth is characterised by a high degree of structural complexity and self-organisation. Such open systems are referred to as "autopoietic", a Greek word meaning "self-producing". This is in opposition to machines which are allopoietic, i.e., are produced by others (Maturana, 1978; Varela and Maturana, 1981). Autopoietic systems have semi-permeable boundaries and are essentially self-relating, and are not readily understood in terms of simple linear causality. It is more useful to see them operating as part of a more complex systemic circular causality. This also pertains to humans, our nervous systems and genomes. We now take a closer look at humans and how change may come about by means of psychotherapy in the light of the above understandings of evolution.

24 Relevance to Psychotherapy

The juxtaposition of aetiology and teleology is also clearly relevant to psychotherapy. As mentioned earlier, most schools of psychotherapy have assumed an aetiological perspective. For behaviourists, this is mainly described in terms of one's history of conditioning and reinforcement. Cognitive therapists focus on past acquisitions of inappropriate or unhelpful cognitions. Psychoanalysts emphasise the importance of infantile instinctual drives, desires, motives, defences, deficits, complexes and unresolved conflicts in the genesis of the neuroses. Hence one can note that key psychoanalytical authors like Sigmund Freud (1900, 1930) and Melanie Klein (1946a) took an aetiological position in which the "push" of innate instincts, drives and unconscious fantasies play determining roles (Fisher and Greenberg, 1996). For Freud, non-dual or "oceanic", spiritual experiences of wholeness, completeness and fundamental connection to something greater were interpreted as a regression to uterine and early-life experiences of fusion with the mother. Here Freud was making the common mistake of confounding trans-verbal (spiritual) with pre-verbal (infantile) states – what philosopher Ken Wilber has identified as the pre/trans fallacy (Wilber, 1996).

However, from early on there has been some opposition to the traditional, purely dualistic aetiological view – with its attendant "backward elaboration" in praxis (e.g. Kelly, 1955). Few people would dispute the importance of proximate aetiological factors on current behaviour, but clinicians like Carl Jung (1958), stressed the importance of teleological and collective factors in our attitudes and behaviours, and how we become more aware of these as we approach mid-life.

Unlike Freud, who became an atheist, Jung was not willing to explain all human behaviour in terms of early ontogeny, i.e. in terms of our psychosexual motives, conflicts and developmental arrests. Jung's view incorporated both aetiological and teleological influences. He emphasised both the "push" of archetypes (phylogeny) in the context of a wider collective unconscious, balanced by their "pull" towards self-actualisation and a search for spiritual meaning (*Mythos*), with all of these together forging the human condition. For Harari (2014, 2015) we humans are the supreme, if not unique, myth-making, storytelling form of life. In the Jungian sense, we can envisage the field of the collective unconscious (an aspect of "universal mind"?) interacting with our personal minds or psyches (and thus also with our bodies) to shape and express our evolving humanity and concomitant myth-making as in philosophy, religion, metaphysics and the like.

British psychoanalyst Wilfred Bion (1970) had a similar vision in that he postulated that thoughts use thinkers to think them – and that this was all occurring in the context of an "ultimate reality" (p.80) or an "absolute truth" (p.117) – which ostensibly could encompass the concept of "universal mind". Here we see echoes of "Platonic Ideas". For Plato with his "Theory of Forms", certain philosophical concepts, e.g. the "Good", "Justice", "Love", "Beauty" and "Truth" exist outside of time, meaning they are eternal (Jowett, 1888). Individual consciousness, through meditation, mindfulness and awareness practices, can evolve in sophistication in order to be able to more fully appreciate these metaphysical concepts.

Many other authors and clinicians have, like Jung, also focussed on the importance of our quest for more rational meaning (*Logos*) as well as for self-actualisation (e.g. Frankl, 1967; Maslow, 1968). George Kelly (1955) based his Personal Construct theory and practice as a clinical psychologist on a human desire to predict the future. His fundamental postulate was that "a person's processes are psychologically channelled by the ways in which he anticipates events" (Kelly, 1955, p.46). Kelly stressed that behaviour was more often "in quest" rather than in response to stimuli.

Being reflective and seeking a purpose which transcends our personal incarnations, is a central theme in the writings of psychotherapists like Carl Jung (1958), George Kelly (1955), Roberto Assagioli (1965), Abraham Maslow (1968), Viktor Frankl (1967) and Wilfred Bion (1970) – to name but a few. These authors incorporate a teleological perspective in that they envisage the "pull" of the future (and of a greater reality) being central to making sense of our existences. This perspective is somewhat more compatible with Wallace's, than with Darwin's, views on evolution.

However, the recent focus on evolutionary genetics and sexual selection has often, but not invariably, been coupled with a form of radical materialism which eschews inquiry into deeper meaning. Those stances to health and well-being which carry the message that life (and evolution) has no meaning beyond genes reproducing themselves ("selfish gene" reductionism) are doing a disservice to patients who are trying to make sense of their experiences but nevertheless feel stuck and unable to do so. Humans are now described as being controlled by bio-algorithms which are largely unconscious, thus depriving us of free-will (Harari, 2015). So, between genetic determinism, neuro-reductionism and environmental forces, there is not much room for freedom of thought or action. Are we thus just bio-robots?

Could it be that one factor in the recent rise in suicides in the Western world is that people are increasingly being exposed to an absurd reductionist scientific culture which conveys the message that our existence is a meaningless bio-chemical "accident", blindly driven by "selfish genes" ending in nothingness? Do some clinicians, albeit unwittingly, further contribute to this *reductio ad absurdum* nihilism by conveying a similar pessimistic message? Arthur Schopenhauer, a great philosophical pessimist of the 19th century, was on the same wavelength as Dawkins. He argued that there is no purpose to existence and that we are all heading nowhere in particular. We are simply tricked by our instincts to reproduce.

As already mentioned, Skinner (1971) argued against the existence of free will, as he saw all behaviour as being entirely determined by both genes and environmental conditioning. The continued popularity of his approach and also that found in other writers such as Dawkins (*"The God Delusion"*, 2006), the emphasis on our "selfish" genes (Dawkins, 1976), our "mean" genes (Burnham and Phelan, 2001) and the conclusion that evolution means that we are soul-less algorithmic organisms (*"Homo Deus"*, Harari, 2015) reflect the nihilistic and narcissistic *Zeitgeist* against which we must struggle in order to make sense of our own experiences and those of our patients. Is this a factor in the increasing level of defeatist depression in the West? Besides the various therapies, could creative, artistic or symbolic expression be an antidote, among others, to depression – expression versus depression!?

Neo-Darwinian perspectives have increasingly been influencing all aspects of Western society. We live in a world where the focus is largely on narcissistic individualism, competition, optimal performance, winning, aggressive marketing, hostile take-overs, etc. Employees are often described as "high-flyers" or as "losers". The "survival of the fittest" mentality is most obvious in the business and banking worlds, but is also increasingly penetrating education (e.g. "league tables") and health services where the "audit culture" means universities and hospitals are more and more being run like businesses and required to turn a profit. Is there really parity of esteem, or even a place, in this neo-Darwinian society for "losers" (including non-conformists), or has neo-Darwinian pessimism won the day? There is evidence of increased (doubled) psychiatric morbidity in nations characterised by "selfish capitalism" such as the USA and the UK, as opposed to those practising "unselfish capitalism" in some parts of mainland Europe (James, 2007).

There has been some concern at the growing influence of neo-Darwinian Theory on psychotherapy practice (DelMonte, 1998a, 1998b, 2001a, 2005, 2011a; Ryle, 2005). If we accept the "selfish-gene" view of primacy of matter over mind (i.e. that mind is solely a by-product of evolved living matter via natural selection) and that Darwinian-inspired theory is adequate to explain the evolution of life and consciousness, then it logically follows that distal and proximate aetiological causes explain all human phenomena (Dawkins, 2006) – including our psychopathology. But can such aetiology really explain our complex subjectivity, existentialist concerns and our quest for meaning? Should we not also include teleological "causality" as well, so as to embrace circular "causality" as advocated within dynamic systems theory?

Looking at causality as being circular, rather than linear, has implications for therapy praxis. With linear causality the relationship between matter and mind is either "bottom up" or "top down". If the relationship between mind and body is in *both* directions then so can be the genesis of illness and its treatment (DelMonte, 1996; Browne, 2013; Halpin, 2014). Many Western psychologists tend to give priority to the mind – as exemplified by the practice of psychotherapy (especially cognitive therapy), which is largely a "mind over matter" approach using prescribed self-verbalisation and the like. But if mind is completely secondary to matter, i.e. no more than emergent from our operative physical brains, then models which emphasise "cerebral over-ride", the "power of positive thinking" or "mind over matter" are fundamentally incompatible with such biological determinism. Yet we know that our minds and bodies are affected by suggestions, hypnosis, expectancy and placebos. These well-established effects are difficult to explain from a purely materialistic perspective and require a deeper understanding of consciousness than is usually found in medical journals. Nor can dualism explain how mind interacts with matter as according to the dualist viewpoint, mind and matter are entirely separate domains.

The "cognitive restructuring" of cognitive therapy, the suggestions given during hypnosis and the "talking cure" of psychoanalysis would, with the materialist perspective, be of limited value, because mind in a linear sense is only secondary to matter. If we are to believe Skinner (1971), there is no such thing as free will. How can there be, if we are wholly determined by both our genes (phylogeny) and our conditioning (ontogeny)? Can (secondary) mind emergent from (primary) matter manipulate this matter, that is, one's emotions and behaviour? With biological linear determinism, there is little scope for an appeal to a reflective, nuanced, inter-subjective, non-dualistic, circular, spiritual or transcendent aspect of mind to inspire and transform us. But what about our scientific, artistic and philosophical creativity: what inspires these? Can personal mind access transpersonal truths? Can personal mind (e.g. one's verbalisations and attitudes) influence the brain (matter) of another person? Well, yes! Magnetic resonance imaging studies show that mother-infant and therapist-patient dyadic interactions can literally alter the orbito-frontal system (Schore, 1994, 2003) in what appears to be inter-subjective resonance (empathy) via "mirror" neurones. In other words, inter-subjective relationships can induce developmental and structural changes in the brain. So, one's mind may not be so purely "personal" after all, and not fully confined to the private workings of one's own physical brain.

Other approaches to well-being, mostly but not exclusively Eastern, focus more on fostered silence and the stillness of meditation, mindfulness and contemplative states. The harnessed and receptive mind resonates in the body, and the trained body in turn affects the mind, as in Zazen, Yoga, Aikido and Qi-gong (DelMonte, 1995b, 1998a, 1998b). One's relationship to time and space becomes unimportant during deep meditation, as one experiences the silent unity of the here and now (DelMonte, 1995b). Does this radical "dwelling in the present" during meditation facilitate a glimpse at the non-dualistic timelessness and spacelessness that was present before the Big Bang?

Systemic-constructivist psychotherapists envisage the relationship between psyche and soma – as well as that between minds – as circular (DelMonte, 1989a, 1989b, 1996, 2009). Here they may agree with Buddhists (and by retro-extension with Hindus) who also hold the view that, ultimately, dualistic "personal mind" (a chip off the "collective mind" block), although socially very useful and narcissistically seductive, is no more than a window (usually with its blinds closed!) onto "universal mind". Moreover, personal mind, the Freudian psyche, is subjected to distortions due to our psychological defences and thus to unconscious influences, as well as to systemic pressures. Eastern practices of mindfulness teach us to observe the transience and ethereality of the personal self, rather than identifying with it, as is the traditional position in Western psychology. Learning to move beyond the everyday, chattering mind to the experience of dimensionless peace, tranquillity and clarity that can be found in meditation allows us to glimpse at the potential for "universal mind" that we harbour within. It helps us see a bigger picture and gain a sense of the possibility for experiencing deeper meaning, as well as a more liberating and less constricted sense of self.

Overall it is difficult to avoid the observation that over time, there has developed a growing awareness of, and concern for, the more vulnerable in society, demonstrating that it is not all about the survival of the fittest. Owning slaves is no longer considered acceptable, nor is discrimination on the basis of race, ethnicity, class, gender, sexual orientation or religion. There is a greater respect for diversity, equality and human rights. The domination of women by men is on the decline and the exploitation of children has lessened. There is also a greater awareness that animals should not be subjected to unnecessary suffering. In brief, over the centuries there appears to be an evolving awareness of, and respect for, the internal emotional world, vulnerability and rights of others, be they foreigners, children, animals, slaves, etc. There shall always be temporary disturbing setbacks but overall, in the longer term, these evolving positive trends are likely to continue. Our ethical development appears to go in hand with an evolution of our capacity for the mental representation of the world around us.

25   Conclusions

So why did our barren rocky Earth eventually produce self-conscious life, musicians, philosophers and psychotherapists, as well as scientists capable of visiting our neighbouring rocky outpost – the moon? In making sense of our lives, aetiology, with both its distal roots in evolution (phylogeny) and its proximate triggers in life events (ontogeny), can usefully be enriched by a teleological perspective (such as Wallace's cosmic causality) with its implied search for purpose and meaning in our individual and collective lives. Wallace's vision of natural selection and evolution may yet prove to be at least as inspiring to us as Darwin's erudite but singular aetiological focus. The natural selection of mutant genetic variants and their developmental epi-genetic expression may ultimately be influenced by, or subject to, fundamental universal laws (of physics, chemistry, consciousness, "non-local mind", etc) in the evolution of conscious life. New mutations may thus be largely predictable at the macro (cosmic) level, whilst appearing to be somewhat "random", hazardous or accidental at the human level. They may also, according to Heisenberg's Uncertainty Principle, appear chaotic at the micro level of sub-atomic particles. This "uncertainty" or randomness yields the variability so necessary to evolution and to individual differences. But it is not an unlimited randomness, as it is bounded within the parameters of the laws of physics (DelMonte, 2011a; Reeves, 2011). In other words, the details of our lives are not completely determined. We have a measure of freedom of choice, as there are some degrees of freedom within a largely structured universe.

Nevertheless, given that the scientifically mysterious "dark matter" and "dark energy" constitute about 96% of our universe (Matthews, 2005) we may have a very long way to go in fully unravelling the mysterious forces involved in evolution and consciousness. Much remains to be elucidated and new discoveries may be "around the corner". But so far, our scientific findings only apply to the four percent of our universe composed of "normal" matter and energy. Our understanding of cosmology is still far too limited. Much remains to be elucidated. Take for example our universe. What was there before the Big Bang?

Is our universe finite? If so, what lies beyond its boundaries? Our universe is apparently expanding more and more rapidly – but into what? Moreover, it is possible that we humans shall never achieve scientific certainty about why life and consciousness evolved as we, like all mammals, may be perceptually and cognitively too limited to ever find out! Maybe the scientific approach cannot answer all questions. Hence the tendency to speculate metaphysically, even though metaphysical postulations cannot deliver certainty either. Living with this uncertainty, with mystery and a "don't-know mind", could be our existential and spiritual challenge, as the origin of life and consciousness may be as much beyond our conceptual grasp as is "ultimate reality". Only scientific and religious fundamentalists try to reduce the truth of evolution, life and consciousness to what our limited senses can apprehend and to what our, often dogmatic, thinking can construe. Thus scientific "how" questions are usefully balanced by philosophical (e.g. existential) "why" ponderings. This is also applies to the theory and practice of psychotherapy, meditation and mindfulness, as one struggles to make sense of our existences, especially in the context of what we choose to do with the range of freedom available to us. These topics are taken up further in Chapters Two, Three and Four of this book.

CHAPTER 2

Awareness: Constructivist, Psychodynamic and Eastern Perspectives

1 Introduction

The traditional split in Western consciousness between the mind and the body has, in recent decades, begun to be healed. For instance, the advent of Eastern practices such as yoga, Tai Chi, acupuncture and macrobiotics have demonstrated how physical interventions can have a profound and positive effect at an emotional and psychological level.

In psychology, the psychodynamic approaches of Freud and the post-Freudians, followed later by the constructivist theories of George Kelly (1905–1967), present complementary models for understanding how consciousness inhabits both the body (soma) and the mind (psyche). Our bodies can express emotions that we perhaps do not have ready access to in our conscious minds. Our somatic experiences are often pre-verbal – like having a "feeling in our gut" that someone cannot be trusted, or developing a bad cold on the day we have to visit our in-laws. The work of therapy often entails helping clients find the words to accurately "name" their experiences, so that the somatic, unconscious material can be brought into consciousness and processed. It is not unusual for clients to overcome long-term conditions such as chronic back pain, migraine or asthma in the course of therapy, as the body's need to express buried feelings through illness becomes redundant when the emotional burdens are identified, expressed and released.

2 Language and Awareness

One could argue that the capacity for the symbolism of sophisticated language is the crucial defining feature that separates humans from the animal world out of which we evolved. As human self-awareness developed over many millennia, language evolved and created a bridge between our inner life and other people, allowing us to share our private thoughts and feelings. Language gives us a potential for communication, creativity and expression that is less developed outside of human society. Every time we make a sentence, we are creating something new.

Language gives us the capacity to transform our experiences symbolically, creating the possibility for transcendence of our instinctive, unconscious evolutionary heritage. Freud said that civilisation began the first day that someone threw an insult instead of a rock. Without language, the highly-complex and sophisticated society and culture we know today could never have evolved.

But as with all evolutionary leaps, the development of language came with a price – the potential of alienation from oneself. Symbolisation through language means that we are one step away from our immediate experience, with a subtle shift towards living "in our heads" rather than living "in our bodies". Particularly in Western culture, the intellectual, the rational and the scientific have come to be highly prized, whilst the humanities, the arts, physical labour and creative expression are seen as secondary (Robinson, 2006).

One of the challenges for the "talking cure" of psychotherapy is to facilitate the client to integrate the relationship between the body and language, using language to acknowledge and express feelings without losing that essential connection to somatic and emotional experience. Developing psychological insight and awareness can liberate people from the tyranny of being driven by their subliminal distress patterns. Bringing repressed unconscious material into consciousness through verbalisation helps repair psychological splits and decreases inner conflicts and tensions, which can otherwise be destructively expressed psychosomatically, in and through the body. As insight and self-awareness develop in the course of therapy, clients gain more control of their emotional lives, allowing them to act more consciously, effectively and maturely, As Freud succinctly described this transformation of the repressed unconscious: "Where Id was, let Ego be".

3   The Continuum of Experience

In this part of the book, constructivist (Kellian) and psychodynamic (both Freudian and post-Freudian) perspectives are employed to illustrate how reality is experienced at different levels of cognitive awareness. Experience can be understood as occurring along a spectrum from concrete to abstract. Children tend to experience the world in a very concrete, immediate way, not having yet developed the cognitive structures to form abstract or intellectual concepts (Piaget, 1967). As these structures gradually emerge, the child learns to see patterns, articulate thoughts and ideas and form hypotheses about the world. Verbal labelling leads our internal representations of primary reality to become more abstract and symbolic, and allows our psyche to operate at a higher conceptual level.

Verbal symbolisation will always by definition be to some degree inadequate and incomplete – even in adulthood. Our unique experiencing can never be translated into language without being reconstructed and losing some of
its immediacy. For this reason, one of the functions of the non-verbal arts is to
express what is inexpressible through words alone.

But the inability to symbolise one's experience can have more debilitating
consequences too. People who are carrying a burden of repressed material that
has never been articulated through symbolisation such as words, can have a
persistent need to express through the body. This can include somatisation
(physical illnesses and conditions), acting out, acting in, as well as primitive
forms of communication and psychological defences such as hysterical identification, projective identification and/or other forms of basic communication
typically found at the lower levels of awareness. Using both constructivist and
psychodynamic models, this chapter examines how verbalisation can be help-
ful in clinical practice with somatoform disorders, where the client exhibits
unexplained physical and emotional symptoms. Drawing on our understanding of Eastern meditation and mindfulness, the role of our psychological defences in limiting our consciousness is explored, in contrast to the practice of
non-verbal mindfulness which aims at expanding our awareness.

Constructivist and psychodynamic models will shed light on the distortion
of consciousness by these defences – albeit from different perspectives. Both
of these psychotherapy approaches are also concerned with the importance
of increased awareness via insight and are therefore complementary to the
Eastern notion of enhanced awareness through the practice of meditation and
mindfulness.

Potential problems with meditation are discussed, as well as limitations to
the "talking cure". For instance, verbalisation can also be used as a higher order
cognitive defence, as observed in rationalisation, and not just in the higher service of the expansion of awareness. However, it is concluded that all awareness
expanding practices, such as mindfulness and insight psychotherapy, reduce
the need to resort to somatisation and other primitive awareness-distorting
and limiting strategies.

4   The Experience of Meditation

Meditation has been a central feature of all the great Wisdom Traditions of
both East and West, practiced as a means of developing consciousness and
awareness and connecting with the transcendent. The recent surge in popularity of meditation in the West has been the catalyst for countless scientific

studies of its effects. Widely used for stress relief, it also has been shown to have a positive effect on many psychological conditions including insomnia, eating disorders, depression, anxiety, panic and phobic disorders (Walsh and Shapiro, 2006).

For individuals with poor ego-strength, it is usually better to engage in psychotherapy prior to taking up meditation (DelMonte, 1990, 2003). Meditation is more about "fine-tuning" than resolving serious emotional conflicts and deficits. One usually commences meditation with training in concentration ("Samatha") before moving on to mindfulness practice ("Vipassana").

In concentration meditation, by focusing exclusively and repetitively on one meaningless stimulus (for example a mantra or one's breath), contrasts tend to fall away and one's perception of the passage of time becomes distorted. As contrasts are necessary for ordinary sense-making, one is left with little or nothing to construe or "no-thought" if adequately adept (DelMonte and Kenny, 1985a; DelMonte, 1987, 2004). This is the nothingness of the *via negativa*. Sustained "nothingness" can lead to an ineffable and non-dualistic transcendental state of non-grasping and equanimity, in which one experiences existential "symmetry", in other words, undifferentiated unity, which for some is the Infinite (DelMonte, 1995b). This is just one example of how meditation practice is embedded in mysticism and spirituality. Samatha means tranquillity or serenity in Sanskrit and Pali.

Having learned to concentrate, it becomes easier to practice Vipassana. Mindfulness meditation promotes the characteristics of an elevated observer status in the here and now, associated with increased reflexivity, vigilance, circumspection and introspection. Put in sensory processing terms, mindfulness meditation involves increased awareness of exteroception (via the five senses), proprioception (via the musculo-skeletal system), and interoception (via the internal organs). In this way, relationships may be noticed between internal and external events, as well as between one's behaviours, bodily processes and cognitions, thereby facilitating the integration of the behavioural, emotional, cognitive and social aspects of our experience (DelMonte, 2003, 2004).

The enhanced mindfulness emergent from Vipassana practice is called "Sati". The knowledge (or enhanced awareness) resulting from Sati is called "Citta". Citta may lead to a form of non-dissociative awareness ("Satipatthana Sutta") where one's consciousness is not split, but rather is integrated holistically, for example, by not "living in one's head" – split off from one's body or from one's surroundings. This is where healing ("making whole") takes place. But achieving non-dissociative awareness is not easy, as consciousness is often split, distorted and reduced (Klein, 1946a), thereby affecting our level of awareness.

5   Maps and Territory: Kelly and Piaget

In our evolutionary history, we probably were sensing, imaging and feeling creatures long before we acquired our current capacity to think and speak. This developmental order also reflects our personal histories, in that language skills take time to develop in a sensate infant. Therefore, ontogenetically (in terms of life-span development) and also phylogenetically (in evolutionary terms), the "thinking-body" is secondarily developed out of the sensory and feeling body (DelMonte, 2005, 2011a). This implies that, in both a developmental and evolutionary sense, imagery and feeling are primary to thinking (in a non-causal way). Thus, our personal history recapitulates our collective history – ontogeny recapitulates phylogeny.

For Kelly (1955) our personal construct systems act as templates or "goggles" through which we perceive and experience the world. Hence, there is no fully objective perception of the world, that is, of primary or ultimate reality. As people move along the dimension of time, they modify their personal constructions of reality so as to be able to anticipate more accurately the cutting edge of the present as they move into the future. Psychological construct systems are personal inner schemas ("maps") that, ideally, are updated from time to time to produce a better fit with the external world (the "territory").

In other words, the construct systems of psychologically adapting individuals are constantly being revised (or rather "accommodated") in the light of newly "assimilated" evidence from the ever-changing world of primary reality (Piaget, 1967). Such perceptual "assimilation" and cognitive "accommodation" à la Piaget of our construct systems allows for a better fit with the flux of primary and social reality. However, such adjustments to our internal worlds, namely to secondary or apparent "reality", are far from straightforward. They are complicated by what we will not or cannot readily face or comprehend, as well as by what is not yet in our awareness – the unconscious.

6   Levels of Awareness: Kelly and Freud

For Freud the repressed unconscious lies, in normal circumstances, below our awareness (Freud, 1900, 1912, 1930). The only two other awareness categories that he envisaged were the conscious and the pre-conscious. George Kelly, a constructivist, saw the range from the unconscious to full consciousness in much more nuanced terms, that is, in terms of a continuous spectrum of levels of cognitive awareness (Kelly, 1955). These levels of awareness were influenced by several factors. These include the degree to which the experiences, of which one is trying to make sense, are somatic, sensory, pre-verbal or have to varying degrees been verbalised as cognitive constructs in language. Some somatic functions may never become verbalisable (the non-verbal domain) and remain fully unconscious and can be referred to as the non-repressed unconscious (such as thermo-regulation, osmo-regulation, immuno-regulation and other bodily, homeostatic functions). On the other hand, the repressed unconscious was once conscious but has been rendered unconscious defensively (Freud, 1900, 1912). According to Schwartz (2000) only between one and five percent of our mental functioning becomes conscious, with the rest of it remaining below conscious access.

Moreover, reality is experienced polymorphically at different levels along a concrete-abstract continuum. At the more abstract, or psychic, level the internal representations of reality become, to varying degrees, verbally labelled. However, this verbal symbolisation is by definition inadequate and incomplete, hence the persistent need for other forms of symbolisation such as found in the arts (for example with music, painting, sculpture and dance). Somatisation and "body language" also fill the gaps of incomplete symbolisation, but at a more concrete level. Somatisation, being a developmentally more primitive form of expression, is more common in childhood, but is also found in adults who have problems in developing symbolic representations. This ability is central to more mature mentalisation, such as found in empathy, so its impairment contributes to a range of psychological disorders (Fonagy et al., 2011). Before exploring more fully these disorders, it is useful to look more deeply at polymorphic reality.

7   Reality: Kelly and Lacan

In our daily lives, the world can be dealt with at different levels of abstraction, ranging from a very concrete and practical level to varying levels of subjective and abstract representation. Furthermore, George Kelly (1955) saw us as living in two realities – firstly the primary or external reality which lies beyond direct and complete human perception, and secondly our attempted interpretations, representations or internal constructions of this primary reality. Likewise, the French psychoanalyst, Jacques Lacan (1966) theorised that we have to deal with three domains or registers – the "Real", the "Imaginary" and the "Symbolic". Lacan's "Real" roughly corresponds to Kelly's primary reality, which is not directly knowable, as ultimate reality can only be dimly perceived indirectly, through our limited senses and cognitions. Lacan's "Imaginary" is somewhat akin to Kelly's notion of attempted internal cognitive construing or attempted representation of this primary reality (the intra-psychic). The "Symbolic" in Lacan's taxonomy pertains to the inter-psychic social domain and to one's attempted adjustment to, and communication within, the external social order in which we are immersed. Such social intercourse is primarily conducted by means of language, but also by using other forms of symbolisation such as art, sculpture, drawing, flags, dress codes and so forth.

For Kelly (1955), we are like "scientists" developing speculative "psychological constructs" (or hypotheses) in order to make sense of the apparent world, by looking for repetitive patterns of similarity and difference among a series of objects or events observed through time. Even as infants, before we acquire language, we construe events dichotomously via bi-polar discriminations such as "milk versus not milk", "mother versus other", "edible versus inedible", "thick versus thin", "hot versus cold", "fair versus unfair" and so on. These psychological constructs, or discriminations, are initially pre-verbal and pre-symbolic (i.e. pre-linguistic), but the growing child in acquiring language comes to attach verbal labels to many such sensory discriminations.

However, much of adult construing remains non-verbal, emotionally unconscious and thus somatic. Throughout one's life, based on one's experiences, one develops and updates one's personal construct system to be used in the anticipation of all types of events (Kelly, 1955). Part of the work of psychotherapy is to uncover and reveal the unquestioned, automatic constructions that inform and even dictate our interactions with others and the world around us. Once made conscious as feelings, outdated and inaccurate constructs, such as a global fear of authority or distrust of women, can be verbally labelled, reconstructed and replaced with more accurate, valid and flexible constructs.

8   Group Construing

Our constructions, or internal representations, of external reality are not just "personal" or construed in isolation. They are also social, in that we develop our construct systems in the context of significant others, such as our parents, siblings, friends, lovers, colleagues, etc. In other words, the social "Symbolic Order" into which we are born (Lacan, 1966) plays a pivotal role in the development of our internal representations of external events.

So it is not just isolated individuals who construe. Kelly (1955) in his "Social Corollary" acknowledged the social aspect of sense-making. Nor is it just humans who need to make discriminations. In the absence of language, a capacity for collective identification allows groups of animals to behave as if they had a "group mind" (McDougall, 1921), as found in shoals of fish, flocks of birds or sheep, and hives of bees and termites. In this way they can share perceptions and feelings – for example of food and danger. Humans, although retaining this capacity for "collective cognition" (Couzin, 2008), do not need to rely on either group or "hysterical" (affective) identifications in order to share information and feelings, to feel empathy or to show compassion and sympathy. They also learn to communicate, i.e. use language in a social context. In order to talk about experiences (for example, feelings of anger, envy, fear or nausea) we need to use symbolic labels by putting verbal form on feelings. The usage of such labels means that much of primary sense-making acquires a secondary (cognitive or more abstract) overlay. The emergence of this cognitive overlay, or symbolic representation, also facilitates the emergence of empathy, which is an essential feature of mentalisation.

Mentalisation is defined as the ability to make and use mental representations of one's own and other people's emotional states. It involves being able to recognise, name and interpret one's deeper emotions as they emerge into consciousness as feelings, thereby allowing appropriate regulation of one's "gut" feelings and reactive emotional responses. This also includes being able to "read" and understand the feelings of others, so that one responds appropriately and effectively in social situations. Inadequate parenting and/or childhood trauma can impair the development of mentalisation, which has negative implications for the adult's sense of self, ability to form attachments and adjustment to psycho-social reality (Fonagy et al., 2011).

The Kellian dialectic of pre-verbal construing versus cognitive construing has considerable overlap with the Freudian dichotomy of primary process versus secondary process mentation, with primary process being characterised by non-verbal id drives, instincts and raw emotions, whilst secondary process involves our more rational and language-based ego functioning (Freud, 1912, 1930). Another parallel is with Bion's (1970) raw cognitively unprocessed "beta" elements and with his more cognitively processed "alpha" functioning. The former beta elements largely correspond to Kelly's pre-verbal construing, and alpha functioning more to Kelly's cognitive construing. As already mentioned, Kelly (1955) sees the individual as initially constructing his or her own reality at the pre-verbal level and then increasingly going on to construct a sense of reality at the level of (social) linguistic symbolism – namely by developing cognitive constructs (or secondary process mentation in Freudian terms). Hence, in a social context, the "talking body" is seen to be emergent out of a more primitive sensory-affective condition typical of childhood.

In evolutionary terms both projective identification (being unconsciously influenced by another person's largely unconscious prompts) and "hysterical" identification (e.g. taking on the bodily distress of a significant other), as

well as "languaging", are adaptive insofar as they facilitate some level of communication. The difference is that speech operates at a more abstract level
of symbolism and represents an adaptation into the "Symbolic Order" à la
Lacan (1966), whereas both hysterical and projective identification operate
at a lower level of cognitive awareness and tend to remain pre-verbal and less
rational.

However well Lacan's "Imaginary" domain is implicated in our intra-psychic
imaginative construing, and the "Symbolic" in our inter-psychic communications, they can never fully overlap with the "Real" domain ("the ultimate territory") beyond our direct grasp.

9   The Unconscious

It is interesting to note the lay person's lack of enthusiasm for the Freudian concept of "the unconscious". Many go on referring to the "subconscious". This may
be indicative of a preference for a concept which is more nuanced, less sharply
delineated, or less "black or white". Popular views of the "subconscious" tend
to be confused with repressed unconscious material à la Freud (1912). Hence
Kelly (1955) emphasised the importance of "levels of cognitive awareness" in
his Personal Construct Theory. These levels of cognitive awareness can be seen
as an elaboration of Freud's notion of the pre-conscious, but also as including
layers within the unconscious.

Others (e.g. Epstein, 1983) have followed Kelly's lead in emphasising the importance of the pre-conscious, which is a complex but neglected area much in
need of descriptive elaboration. Freud's view of the unconscious and, especially, the pre-conscious is thus replaced by Kelly's (1955) usage of the following
theoretical counterparts, among others: "pre-verbal construing", "suspension",
"submergence", "constriction" and "loosening".

10   Pre-Verbal and Somatic Construing

Kelly used the expression "pre-verbal construing" to cover a broad spectrum within all non-verbal sense-making. Non-verbal constructs are those
perceptual-emotional discriminations that one "sub-consciously" makes
which have not been verbally labelled. Consequently, they are often at a low
level of cognitive awareness and are largely sensed by us as "gut-feelings", intuitions, vague elusive sensations and fleeting impressions – whenever one
tries to become more aware of them. Examples of non-verbal construing are

psycho-physiological, kinaesthetic and non-verbalized emotional discriminations. They also include what Polanyi (1959) encompassed within the concept
of "tacit knowledge" (as opposed to formal knowledge), and are typified by the
phrase "we always know more than we can tell". For example, the tacit knowledge required to perform certain skills, such as riding a bicycle or swimming,
is often more complex than we can readily express in terms of formal knowledge. Silent meditation can be seen as a deliberate attempt to experiment with
coming to know our non-verbal construing, which can include our social conditioning.

Knowledge (including memory) which has to be "acted out" in order to be
communicated is usually at a relatively low level of cognitive awareness, as,
for example, with the disturbed behaviour of those people who were sexually
abused in childhood, but who have repressed or suppressed the memory there-
of (DelMonte, 2000a, 2001b). Such people can display symptoms of histrionic or narcissistic personality disorders, such as excessive need for attention,
over-sexualised behaviour, unstable emotionality and inability to form stable
attachments.

Although non-verbal construing tends to represent a low level of awareness,
it is not to be equated precisely with the unconscious. Some non-verbal construing may be communicated (often unknowingly or at the borders of consciousness) by means other than words, as through behavioural "leakage" or in
the non-verbal arts. Such analogical communication stands in sharp contrast
with the more usual digital (or verbal) communication. People often sacrifice
precision of description in order to communicate nebulous feelings which
may otherwise elude expression.

Analogical communication can also be conceptualised as a variant of psychological projection, as it is often picked up by its recipients as vague intuitions and so forth. When the recipient of such projections reciprocates in the
prompted and desired manner, i.e. identifies with it to some degree, then we can
describe this mutuality of feeling and behaviour as "projective identification".
This can occur when, for instance, a person with a strong unconscious need
to control marries a spouse who is terrified of autonomy and unconsciously
wishes to be taken in charge or controlled. It tends to be a pre-conscious (i.e., a
"sub-conscious") – or even an unconscious mutuality. It is commonly found in
mother-infant relationships and among lovers, but often also, as transference,
in psychotherapy dyads and in group therapy.

Pre-verbal constructs are those non-verbal constructs which have not yet
been verbally labelled but which, in general, are potentially capable of labelling. Insofar as most non-verbal constructs arise in pre-linguistic childhood and
remain poorly verbalised (that is barely symbolised) they can also be referred

to as sub-verbal constructs. When our sense-making discriminations become verbally labelled through speech they can be seen as cognitive (or verbal) constructs, whereas somatic construing tends to remain relatively unverbalised as in unconscious homeostasis and emotion. Basic aspects of somatic construing include posture, balance, osmo-regulation, thermo-regulation, somatic reflexes and the like. Somatic construing also includes the discriminations which one makes in terms of one's instincts and drives, such as is found with a range of compelling attractions – what we like and dislike. In order to talk about our emerging emotions (for example feelings of anger, envy or disgust) we need to use verbal labels. The usage of such labels means that much of our construing (ego functioning) has both somatic and cognitive components. This is why for Freud (1900, 1912, 1930) the ego is primarily a bodily ego, and only secondarily a cognitive one

By now it should be clear that in understanding Kelly's (1955) theory it is important not to confound construing with mere verbal formulation. Whilst some construing becomes formulated in symbolic speech, this is only the "tip of the iceberg". Much of non-verbal construing or discriminating can be seen in psycho-physiological terms having to do with phenomena such as pain, blood pressure responses, neuro-muscular effects, endocrinological secretions, immune responses, gastro-intestinal reactions, kinaesthetics and the like. Such non-verbal and sub-symbolic processing has already been referred to as somatic construing. It literally plays a "vital" role in our self-organisation. Here, Kelly's position is remarkably close to Freud's who, as already mentioned, saw the ego as being primarily a somatic ego.

The sense-making of most sub-human animals is largely confined to primitive somato-sensory construing, which in perceptual terms can be referred to as proprioception (perception of the position and posture of the body in space), interoception (perception of the internal systems of circulation, digestion, excretion, etc) and exteroception (perception of the external world).

As already mentioned, pre-verbal constructs originated mostly in infancy in order to make sense of those elements of life encountered by the infant in its growth and development. When people get into difficulty using their adult constructs, their first defence typically is "hostility" to invalidating evidence (Kelly, 1955). However, a later defence is often regression to the pre-verbal constructs of infancy, for example, to extreme dependency and emotive "outbursts". Hence, we often find psychosomatic symptomatology and "cries for help" accompanying strong unfulfilled dependency needs. Conversion or histrionic symptomatology, on the other hand, often symbolises strong unconscious conflicts and identifications (Freud, 1900, 1912, 1930) as, for example, found in phantom pregnancy, histrionic immobility and histrionic blindness.

11   Suspension

This constructivist notion is used by Kelly (1955) to encompass defences nor-mally referred to by a broad range of terms such as "forgetting", "repression" and "dissociation" in psychoanalytic theory. Suspension (holding in abeyance) normally means that certain experiences or "elements" are temporarily placed outside the scrutiny of one's conscious construct system because of incompat-ibility with the overall system a person is currently using. Hence defensively suspended elements are usually at a relatively low level of cognitive awareness and are not readily tested out against apparent reality.

But not all suspension is defensive as it can also be adaptive. In terms of the detached attitude that Samatha meditators learn to take towards the various elements entering their awareness, one may describe this concentrative prac-tice as a deliberate, short-term, adaptive suspension – or adaptive dissociation in Freudian terms. Such a suspension of habitual cognitive construing has also been described as "de-automatisation" (DelMonte, 1990, 1995a, 2003).

In Kellian terms, de-automatisation implies the construing of reality afresh without our biased "perceptual goggles" or psychological filters. For Kelly (1955) this would have been well-nigh impossible as conclusions are likely to be arrived at according to one's perceptual prejudices and expectations. Such biases are likely to be associated with resistance to invalidating evidence (Kel-lian defensive "hostility"). On the other hand, mindfulness meditation (Vipas-sana) is ostensibly characterised by enhanced receptivity, or to use construct terms, by an increased openness or permeability of one's construct system to new ideas (or "elements" à la Kelly). Mindfulness meditation can provide an opportunity for *post hoc* falsifiable experimentation (Popper, 1959) in which old constructs are more open to the validational fortunes presented by the ex-periential flux of reality. Hence, mindfulness ostensibly fosters reality testing while temporarily holding one's habitual prejudices (pre-judgements) in abey-ance – in so far as this is possible. The suspension referred to during mind-fulness practice is volitional and potentially adaptive. Habitual construing is suspended, including our more conscious defensive constructions. As a conse-quence, previously suppressed (suspended) unprocessed material may come to the fore during meditation, referred to as "unstressing" (abreaction) when it is emotionally laden.

With mindfulness practice, meditators see themselves and their thoughts as elements which are observed in a detached or rather a non-attached and non-judgemental way. This can be described as "bare-witnessing", when one prac-tises observation without an internal running commentary. Moreover, the non-evaluative free-flowing attention, or "choiceless awareness" (Krishnamurti,

1991) of mindfulness meditation involves, rather like in free association, the unhindered and spontaneous flow of images, thoughts and feelings without internal censorship (DelMonte, 2011b). During mindfulness meditation, one is asked to look upon all experience as novel. In this sense one's attention is de-automatised, which is another way of saying that the meditator views the contents of his or her awareness as novel events, free from one's usual biases. In other words, habitual, logical and verbally labelled construing (or Freudian secondary process mentation) is temporarily suspended. As habitual cognitive construing (ordinary thinking) is suspended, there is often recourse to sub-verbal, pre-logical and somatic construing, with the possible liberation of un-processed emotion (or Freudian primary process material).

Depending on what is in his or her sub-verbal reservoir, the meditator becomes in touch with different aspects of the self through experiencing feelings such as fear, anger, anxiety and sexual arousal, or even momentary "no-thought" episodes if the sub-verbal material has been adequately "worked through". The meditator may also experience temporal and spatial distortions and so forth as one experiences the unbounded "here and now" for an extend-ed period. In this way, this "uncovered" or unsuspended self can become part of the conscious self.

12   Constriction and Dilation

With constriction, the boundaries of one's perceptual field are deliberately re-duced so that fewer elements are left for construing. Incompatibilities within one's construct system may thus temporarily be minimised. Dilation, on the other hand, involves the deliberate enlargement of one's perceptual field so that more elements are encompassed (Kelly, 1955). This may facilitate a re-organisation of one's construct system at a more comprehensive level. By way of clinical analogy, one can say that depression is largely characterised by cognitive and behavioural constriction – as there are restrictions in activity level, socialising, appetite, libido and the like, whereas elation has features of dilation à la Kelly in that there is a notable expansion in "reaching-out-to-the-world" activities.

In meditation, the re-organisation hoped for is variously termed "enlighten-ment", "nirvana" or "serenity". Dilation, as in mindfulness meditation, involves an expansion of the perceptual field, opening up the mind to new phenomena, flowing from one topic to another, and trying to find new connections between this increased range of events. By taking a more distant perspective on these varieties of experience, one may be able to abstract or perceive similarities and differences among them, and thereby build bridges between the events by making new connections. In the opposite direction, namely that of constriction (as in concentration meditation), the meditator limits his or her focus of interest, tending to deal with only one issue at a time, often in the form of a mantra or another object of concentration. The person here is dealing with a much reduced psychological universe.

From a Kellian point of view, concentrative meditation is a deliberate experiment with constriction of the perceptual field. What are the consequences of reducing the number of elements to be dealt with to one bi-polar element which needs little construing – as with a mantra versus no mantra or inhaling versus exhaling? In this form of meditation, a deliberate attempt is made to disrupt and displace usual logical sense-making. Continuous focusing on only one element means that construing is very focused, concrete, repetitive and controlled. As a result, verbally-labelled cognitive construing (more typical of the left hemisphere) is blocked, disrupted or curtailed so that the mind resorts to sub-verbal and pre-cognitive sense-making. Put psychodynamically, if secondary process mentation (as in rational, verbal or adult-like cognition) is blocked, then there may be recourse to the more elementary primary process mentation. Primary process mentation, which is mainly characterised by non-verbal construing, tends to be visual, spatial, kinaesthetic, emotional, somatic, vegetative and so forth, and is more typical of the right hemisphere (DelMonte, 2003, 2004).

The constant monotonous repetition of a mantra, when coupled with reduced sensory input, may enhance a trance-like condition and regressive mentation during which one's repression barriers are weakened by a reduced ability or desire to marshal the cognitive or intellectual defences of a more alert state. This can lead to "unstressing" (or abreaction) as the meditator experiences a range of feelings (such as shame, anger, sadness, or fear) which emerge from his or her reservoir of past experience, which may include what can be referred to as "somatic memory" or "organ speech". Put in sensorial terms, if exteroception is severely curtailed, then there may be recourse to proprioception and interoception. Other outcomes of such perceptual fixation and monotony may be spatial and temporal distortions or reconstructions of the perceived world (DelMonte, 1990).

When novices engage in very intensive concentrative meditation (Kellian constriction) the outcome is unpredictable and largely depends on the meditators' covert historical repertoires and on recent events ("day-residue" in psychodynamic terms). They may experience "unstressing" as emotional pre-verbal construing takes over (DelMonte, 1987, 1990). Occasionally, they may experience hypnogogic reverie, surrealistic imagery and increased suggestibility if they become relaxed and drowsy (DelMonte, 1981).

The more adept meditators may experience some "no thought" at will during practice. "No thought" is characterised by cognitive quiescence and non-attachment to thoughts, while remaining alert and restful. This may be achieved, in part, because the meditator had "worked through" or emotionally processed defended-against material. It may, however, also be the result of adeptness in using concentration techniques. "No-thought" indicates that functions associated with both brain hemispheres have been deliberately inhibited, resulting in a non-dual state where few or no cognitive discriminations are made. Without dualistic discrimination, we have experiential "symmetry", in that there is no discrimination of opposites or discernment of contrasts. Meditators report subjective feelings of deep harmony, equanimity and a sense of timelessness in these states. This is also a feature of the deep, unrepressed, unconscious (Matte Blanco, 1988).

13   Submergence

We have already referred to the fact that Kelly (1955) sees construing as being bi-polar, for example, love/hatred and weak/strong. However, for some people only one end of the pole is cognitively elaborated – the other end being submerged (often somatically) and therefore largely unconscious – for example, with the cerebrally inclined who also show psychosomatic disorders, or with the covert sadistic tendencies of a masochist, and even with the manipulative power of weakness. Submerged poles also feature in Freudian "reaction formation" when, for example, a homophobic man denies his own homosexual undercurrents. In Taoist philosophy there is always some "Yin" buried in "Yang" and vice versa. In this sense a submerged pole is also akin to Jung's (1958a) notion of the "shadow", especially when the submerged pole is seen to be undesirable. Although influential, the submerged pole is temporarily safe from any direct confrontation with social reality, thus remaining unlikely to be experientially tested out. However, submerged material, i.e. unconscious emotions, may also abreactively emerge during concentrative meditation.

It is worth pointing out that before Kelly's time, both Jung (1958a, 1958b) and Freud (1900) showed interest in duality. The Freudian position is that opposites lie close to each other in the unconscious: in other words, the deeper the unconscious the weaker the duality (Matte Blanco, 1988). With decreasing cognitive awareness, our capacity to construe contrasts and make discrete discriminations weakens, thus the greater the similarity between the poles. This, as already mentioned, is also referred to as unconscious symmetry (Matte Blanco, 1988).

Similar ambivalence often emerges during dreams, meditation and depth psychotherapy, as these may release the dynamic interaction of our polarities, for example, as with confusion between dependence and independence, isolation and fusion, maleness and femaleness, and so forth. Suler (1991) saw a correspondence between psychodynamic views on the human propensity for bi-polar thinking and the ancient Taoist philosophy evoking the Yin and Yang principle in all human discriminating.

Jung's (1958a) concept of *coniunctio* (or the Marriage of Opposites) is relevant here. For example, the experiential tensions between love and hatred, between assertion and submission, between speech versus silence, or between conscious versus unconscious, display oppositional interplays which, by means of Jung's "transcendent function", can be resolved by the creation of new insightful psychic products (Jung, 1958a, p.90; Bravesmith, 2012). Jung's views are somewhat similar to those postulated about five hundred years BC by the Greek philosopher, Heraclitus, with his concept of the "Harmony of Opposites", in that he envisaged a fundamental unity between what appear to be opposite phenomena.

14   Loosening and Tightening

A "loosened" construct system is one marked by degrees of vagueness, diffuseness and uncertainty. A loose construer is someone who cannot "make up his mind", because, in the personal construct sense, much of his or her mind remains vague and elusive, hence at a relatively low level of cognitive awareness. Such looseness is not very good for making firm predictions. Examples of loose construing are to be found in schizoid thinking, free association, dreaming, hypnogogic reverie, poetry and imaginative play; whereas tight construing tends to be logical, analytical, judgemental, legalistic, numerical, computational, scientific and so forth. The essence of loose construing is that it cannot readily be "pinned down" and invalidated. When one thinks loosely, one is protected by a type of elasticity, or resilience, in the face of a threatening reality which might shatter our constructs (i.e. hypotheses) were they any tighter. This is because tighter construing (hypotheses) can be more readily pinned down, put to the test and invalidated. Such invalidating effects, when testing reality, can be emotionally devastating and provoke extreme anxiety. Loosening therefore offers a "shifty defence" (Kelly, 1955, p.1030) against a world which one cannot face. Schizoid thinking appears to be an example of such a defence.

The schizoid personality is emotionally cold and remains detached from interpersonal relations, though the person may appear superficially friendly.

Schizoid thinking, being to some degree cut off from social reality and from internal emotions, is relatively "unanchored". It allows one to make rather loose
connections between one's imagination (Lacan's Imaginary register) and social reality (Lacan's Symbolic register). On the other hand, obsessional thinking is unusually tight and dichotomous ("black or white"), in so far as there is a
particularly narrow focus of attention on specific mental constructs, e.g. clean
versus dirty. With both schizoid and obsessional thinking, there is distorted
and thus impaired consciousness. The essence of creativity, according to Kelly, involves a "to and fro" between loose and tight construing: The looseness
allows for new associations and the tightness for testing these out against apparent reality. This "to and fro" is lacking in people locked into either schizoid
or obsessional defences. Obsessional thinking, being rather tight, often lacks
imagination. Schizoid thinking, being too loose, is untestable. Tight and loose
construing both have their value. In education we tend to focus on tightening,
as, for example, in science and mathematics. However, creative imagination
requires a Yin-Yang type of interplay between looseness and tightness – usually
commencing with the former (Kelly, 1955; DelMonte, 1987, 1995a, 2003).

In psychotherapy, there are a number of ways of producing loosening, including the use of relaxation techniques, free association, dream work, and
by the non-judgemental acceptance of the patient (Kelly, 1955). It is postulated that mindfulness meditation also enhances loosening (DelMonte, 1995a).
Speeth (1982) suggested that mindfulness meditation resembles free association, in that both concern the uncensored or spontaneous loose flow of ideas
and feelings. The same phenomenon occurs during concentrative meditation
on a more limited scale if one temporarily "forgets" to repeat the mantra or to
count one's breath. During mindfulness meditation one is encouraged to adopt
a neutral, or "de-automatised", stance towards all material which comes into
one's awareness (as in Kellian suspension of construing). Meditation often, but
not always, involves a degree of relaxation (DelMonte, 1990) as well as reduced
exteroception. The monotonous repetition of a mantra (as in concentrative
meditation), when combined with reduced sensory input and a shift towards
relaxed para-sympathetic functioning, may encourage hypnogogic reverie.
Hypnogogic reverie, like dreaming, relaxation and free association, is characterised by a loosening of one's personal construct system.

The psychoanalyst's attentive non-judgemental acceptance of the patient's
utterances in psychotherapy is paralleled by the mindfulness meditator's non-
selective and non-judgemental attitude towards the contents of his or her own
mind. This is also ideally required of analysands in "free association", which,
when proceeding well, is also a form of mindfulness practice (DelMonte,
2011b). Moreover, mindfulness meditation appears to be characterised by

factors which, according to Kelly, produce a loosening of one's personal construct system – namely degrees of "relaxation", "free association" and "non-judgemental acceptance".

The value of tight construing, as in physics, law and computer programming, is widely acknowledged. However, loose construing also has several important functions in the psychological life of the person. In general, it facilitates an increasing awareness of hitherto excluded elements. Hence loosening is often encouraged in therapy. For example, in psychotherapy it helps the person to remember forgotten events. Loosening also enables us to perceive "old facts" anew; that is, in a different light. Moreover, loosening tends to expand the construct's range – through increased diffuseness and elasticity. Hence loosening can admit new experiences. By shuffling ideas, it can recombine them into new patterns and also may facilitate the person in coming to verbally express pre-verbal discriminations.

From the above, one can see that loosening has a large role to play in producing new experience. Perhaps in mindfulness meditation (as with free association and relaxation) it is the loosening procedure which puts the person in the way of having an experience (often emotional) which he or she has not had before, maybe via catharsis, or an experience which has the quality of a great "insight". This may be the same type of "flash of inspiration" which creative people are often known to experience – especially while relaxing, for example, as with Archimedes in his bath, Newton under his apple tree and Einstein with his "thought experiments" (Kenny and DelMonte, 1986).

Thus, meditation may be construed as a creative enterprise. The loosening process facilitates an important connection between intuitive creativity and pre-verbal construing, insofar as it may lead to approximate verbalisations for difficult-to-verbalise feelings. As already mentioned, Kelly (1955) tied creativity to a cycle between loosened and tightened construing. The loosening which often occurs during mindfulness meditation may be followed by tightened construing after meditation. In this sense, loosened constructs emergent during meditation can be firmed up as testable hypotheses after the practice of meditation and then subjected to reality testing. Reality testing may confirm or disprove some of the constructs flowing out of meditation practice. In this way, meditation may be seen as a dynamic process where the person's own self is the material which is being innovatively transformed by using material emergent from the unconscious. Here the unconscious is being viewed in the Jungian sense; that is, as potentially nourishing and adaptive, and not just as a reservoir of primitive and disavowed material à la Freud's repressed unconscious (Jung 1958, 1958a). Concentrative meditation may facilitate "creative emptiness" in which "benevolent depersonalisation" is fostered, characterised by the discarding of unhelpful id impulses and super-ego controls (Moncayo, 2003).

It may be that at a certain stage of loosening the person begins to lose his or her system's structure (including one's defences) and it is this loss of structure which Kelly (1955) calls anxiety. Thus it is common for many people engaged in loosening techniques, like meditation and yoga, to experience sudden bursts of anxiety, which may be a measure of the degree of their loosening behaviour and their sense of impending loss of structure. This phenomenon may help to explain other reports of paradoxical anxiety/arousal during relaxation (Heide and Borkovec, 1983, 1984; Norton et al., 1985). The anxiety experienced during loosening techniques such as mindfulness meditation and relaxation may reflect the degree to which the techniques in question have loosened one's cognitive defences.

It may, by now, be apparent that there appear to be similarities between the cathartic release of emotional material found during meditative unstressing and that found in the abreaction of free association. Both may have much in common with the cathartic phenomena found by Grof (1975) in his work with psychedelic drugs and later with his technique of hyperventilation. It may be that these techniques act as "loosening" exercises at the somatic level and facilitate the expression of sub-verbal material. Furthermore, it appears that the above loosening techniques have much in common with the "uncovering" techniques of Gestalt therapy (DelMonte, 1990, 1995a) insofar as they both facilitate access to material at lower levels of awareness. Meditation practice, like regression techniques, can thus lead to the uncovering of unconscious material. However, all forced uncovering techniques, unlike self-paced ones as in psychoanalysis and meditation, carry the risk that clients subjected to them may have some difficulty in dealing with prematurely exposed emotional material unless given adequate support. This is where the Buddhist approach is relevant.

15   Constructivism, Buddhism and Duality

As McWilliams (1984) postulates, both Buddhist Psychology and Kellian Personal Construct Theory acknowledge that normal human understanding of our universe involves the use of dualistic conceptual dimensions to make sense of an ultimately unitary universe. For Kelly (1955) all constructs are bi-polar. Kelly in his theorising developed his own bi-polar constructs to elaborate his Personal Construct Theory, such as "loose" versus "tight", and "constricted" versus "dilated", verbal versus non-verbal, etc.

There is also a long tradition in psychoanalysis of postulating concepts in bi-polar terms. If one can postulate a concept then we can also imagine its opposite. For example, Freud's "pleasure principle" is contrasted with his "reality principle", as is Thanatos, the death instinct, with Eros. This is also true for Freud's "primary process" and his "secondary process" (Freud, 1900, 1912, 1930). Bion (1970) similarly distinguished "alpha" functioning from "beta" elements. Jung also contrasted "anima" with "animus", "introverted" with "extraverted", and "persona" with "shadow" (Jung, 1958, 1958a). Matte Blanco (1988) with his "bi-logic" theory noted that the deep unconscious is characterised by "symmetry" (no contrasts), whereas logical consciousness is "asymmetrical", that is, is characterised by discriminatory construing such as "male versus female", "mother versus wife" and "old versus young". The basic unitary unconscious becomes, by means of dualistic construing, increasingly discriminated and complexified as one becomes more and more conscious – and vice versa as we become less conscious

Melanie Klein saw psychological "splitting" as starting in early infancy and persisting throughout most of life, usually to separate the desirable from the undesirable, for example the "good breast" from the "bad breast" (Klein, 1946). The "bad" is often disavowed and projected psychologically into demonised others. Buddhist approaches would emphasise the need to see through this illusion of duality via practices such as concentrative and mindfulness meditation and universal loving kindness meditation.

16   The Healing Essence of Buddhism

As already alluded to, thinking tends towards dualism. McWilliams (1984, p.2) wrote, "to the extent that we attend to conventional, dichotomous ideas about the universe, we are taken away from direct, immediate experience of the universe". Buddhism, and many Eastern writers such as De Mello (1990), would see suffering as stemming from our desire to force the unitary (inter-penetrating) world to conform to our dualistic and egocentric cravings, beliefs and values. Anxiety and alienation often result from experiencing ourselves as separate from an unpredictable "outside world" that we feel the need to control.

McWilliams contends that the Buddhist viewpoint is that it is possible to transcend the illusion of our self-invented dualistic world. In seeing the transparency of our construct system, we experience a greater sense of unity (with our universe). Such an experience comes from an awareness of how we personally construct our subjective view of this greater ultimate reality. This awareness involves a journey which may be unfolded through the practice of mindfulness meditation and the like.

A fundamental concern about dualistic construing is that it creates conceptual divisions and boundaries in a universe that Buddhists postulate to be inherently holistic and unitary – yet in constant flux rather than static. Concepts tend to fragment reality by discriminating extra layers of asymmetry (differences). Different languages fragment reality in their own unique ways, rendering exact translations between them well-nigh impossible.

Buddhist practices of mindfulness, meditation, the development of insight and ethical living typically put one in touch with compassion and "interbeing", that is, with the inter-penetration and inter-dependence of all forms of life (Thich Nhat Hanh, 1975, 1991, 2003). This can bring about fundamentally liberating changes in one's sense of self: not as a vulnerable, isolated ego in an indifferent world, but as an integrated part of a greater and evolving whole. This relates to the aim of transcendence, when the advanced meditator experiences the undifferentiated unity and "oneness" that lies beyond symbolisation, language and duality (DelMonte, 2003, 2004).

17   Transcendence, Ascendance and Descendance

Kelly (1955) was adamant on the notion of bi-polarity of construing. For Kelly one always abstracts on the basis of both similarity and contrast. Dichotomy is seen as an essential feature and, ultimately, a limitation of thinking itself. Whilst Kelly says that one can transcend one's current biography and not become a victim of circumstance, one can only do this through developing alternative bi-polar constructs. One never escapes from one's construct system, but always assimilates the world through it or through its elaborations.

Thus, when one transcends a particular bi-polarity, one tends to climb up to a higher and more abstract level, but to a level which, nonetheless, is structured in bi-polar terms. Here Kelly was following the 19th century Hegelian dialectic where the creative tension between a thesis and an anti-thesis is seen as potentially producing a synthesis – albeit another bi-polar one! Jung was also inspired by Hegel. As already mentioned, he referred to the creative tension and interplay between binary opposites in producing a synthesis (a new psychic product) as the "transcendent function" (Jung, 1958b, a, p.90). The ancient Taoist Yin-Yang dialectic also springs to mind here, in that it preceded and may well have inspired the theorising of Hegel, Jung and Kelly.

It may be that some meditation and yoga practices are directly or indirectly attempting to elaborate the non-verbal construing of the person so that it undermines the dualistic verbally-labelled constructions. From this point of view, one could initially be talking about "descendance" from the psyche to the soma, rather than transcendence. One, therefore, can distinguish between descendance, ascendance and transcendence. Descendance implies moving "downwards" from cognitive to pre-verbal construing – be it sensory or somatic. In psychodynamic terms this may be characterised by adaptive regression, as opposed to mal-adaptive (e.g. psychotic) regression which is characterised by irrationality. With descendance there may also be a gradual decrease in the level of consciousness into the pre-conscious – right down to the somatic unconscious level.

Ascendance, on the other hand, describes a movement "upwards" to a higher and more abstract bi-polar construct, that is, to super-ordinate construing within one's personal construct system. An example would be learning to appreciate the beauty of sculpture or painting, rather than confining that appreciation to the human body. Freudian "sublimation" of basic instincts and drives comes to mind here. Such super-ordinate construing may, if taken far enough, be seen as an aspect of the supra-conscious (Assagioli, 1965). For Assagioli the super-conscious was a level above ordinary awareness similar to what many Eastern religions refer as "higher consciousness". At this level, it may also become difficult to verbalise one's experiences, or, in other words, to symbolise. An example here could be sexual or romantic love mutating into ineffable (non-dualistic) spiritual love.

Transcendence, as found in "no-thought", is the feeling of unity or bliss when the meditator has the experience that he or she has temporarily transcended the bi-polarity of all cognitive construing – but nonetheless is still construing at a very basic somatic level in terms of balance, posture, respiration, osmoregulation, blood pressure and other vital aspects of one's metabolism. Transcendence is, therefore, where the person recovers his or her non-verbal sense of "oneness" by not confusing the duality of our personal bi-polar construing with the essential unity of greater reality which lies beyond symbolisation.

Paradoxically, both ascendance and adaptive descendance, insofar that they side-step the bi-polar thinking mind, may involve varying degrees of quiescence, the former by superseding the dualistic mind, and the latter by reverting to non-dualistic somatic "just being". In this sense, both ascendance and descendance appear to show aspects of the same unitary circle of life. However, the road to somatic "just being" can be full of pitfalls.

18   Somatoform Disorders

Various factors, such as growing up in an unsympathetic family environment, can lead to distortions in the development of symbolisation and awareness.

We can thus turn to the field of psychosomatic and histrionic disorders where complaints are largely manifested in the somatic format. Patients with psychosomatic symptoms tend to be very concrete in their presentation of complaints, due to a difficulty with verbal symbolisation. Such patients often show varying degrees of alexithymia in that they have difficulty identifying and naming their own feelings and those of others (Vanheule et al., 2011). The word "a-lexi-thymia" comes from ancient Greek and means "without words (for) feelings". Unsurprisingly, this condition invariably leads to inter-personal problems (Vanheule et al., 2010) as not being able to notice, locate, name and communicate feelings in oneself and others handicaps the social self. It can also lead to a range of psychological disorders, including depression and eating disorders (Fonagy et al., 2011).

In discussing disorders involving psychosomatic symptoms, Kelly (1955) illustrates how the "mind-body" construct can be applied pre-emptively by such patients. This is where people often show a strong "mind-body" split. The difficulty lies in both concrete and dualistic thinking. The person is unable to construe herself as a whole because the body is construed in a "mechanical" manner and the area of mind is construed largely in a separate "intellectualized" way (Kelly, 1955, p.921).

A solution, according to Kelly, for overcoming such mind/body dualism is to be found in (adaptive) regression in psychotherapy to early forms of pre-verbal thinking. "Only at that primitive level may we find that the mind and the body were not pre-emptively separated" (p.921). There are several pathways to achieving such adaptive regression – such as in Gestalt therapy, psychoanalysis, meditation and hypnosis (DelMonte, 2011b). For example, in Zen meditation, the use of Koans is an assault on the mind/body dualism found with cerebral defences.

Paradoxically, although an objective of meditation is to move beyond, that is to transcend the habitual state of verbalised consciousness, elements of this dualistic state remain incorporated, intact and available for practical, social and aesthetic usage. However, the meditator now becomes aware of these cognitive dualisms from the perspective of a more neutral and mindful observer, and is less prone to unwittingly over-identify with them. With mindfulness meditation (Vipassana) one strives to achieve non-dissociative (non-split) consciousness by neither clutching onto nor rejecting the fullness of immediate experience, for example by not letting one's attention drift away from one's embodied self while engaging in daily tasks.

As already mentioned, pre-verbal constructs originated mostly in infancy in order to make sense of those elements of life encountered by the infant in its growth and development. When people get into difficulty using their adult constructions, their last line of defence is often maladaptive regression back to the pre-verbal constructions of infancy, with its attendant infantile dependency. Hence we often find psychosomatic symptomatology accompanying strong unfulfilled dependency needs. Histrionic symptomatology, likewise associated with dependency needs, often symbolises strong unconscious conflicts, which one defensively avoids because of inherent feelings of fear, shame or guilt. According to Leader and Corfield (2008) many somatoform symptoms are also associated with strong, largely unconscious, identifications with other people's suffering.

The psychoanalyst Hogan (1995) presents an interesting comparison between histrionic somatoform conversions, which he sees as post-oedipally symbolic, and the more primitive pre-oedipal psychosomatic disorders which, he postulates, operate at a lower (often pre-verbal) level of symbolism, with less conscious control. For Hogan, psychosomatic disease of the gut can either represent psychosexual developmental arrest at the oral-anal (or "gut") phase, or an emotional regression back to that phase, following a perceived threat to one's security. In this respect, Hogan sees the alexithymia of many psychosomatic patients as a defence against the shame felt about negative fantasies and emotions by blocking their conscious emergence and verbalisation. Instead these negative impulses are directed inwards to produce "masochistic gratification in the pain of psychosomatic symptoms" (p.103). This masochism, coupled with alexithymia and/or other defensive postures, makes psychosomatic disorders difficult to treat. So it is to treatment issues that we now return.

19   Catharsis, Insight and Integration

It has been argued by McGee et al. (1984) that emotional experiences which are too threatening to one's core psychological functioning can be defensively suspended or frozen as "un-experienced experiences", in other words, without being emotionally processed or integrated at a conscious level. This phenomenon has also more recently been referred to as defensive "experiential avoidance", and was shown to be correlated with a range of symptoms of psychopathology such as panic, anxiety, depression and PTSD (Keogh et al., 2008).

In a sense, such experiences remain akin to the "unfinished business", the "unfulfilled needs", or the "incomplete Gestalten" referred to by Gestalt therapists. These incomplete Gestalten are usually at low levels of cognitive awareness and tend to be psychologically projected or "acted out" behaviourally, for example hysterically, in order to be communicated – often with considerable feeling but with little rational reflection. In this sense the symptoms of hysteria are seen to be functional and symbolic (Szasz, 1972a).

The weakening of one's cognitive defences during psychotherapy (and during concentrative meditation) facilitates the abreactive emergence of such incomplete Gestalten, as well as of repressed and dissociated material. In other words, the experience which was held in a sort of "suspended animation" can be relived emotionally – initially as "somatic memory", then with hindsight reprocessed and integrated into one's personal construct system at a more insightful level of awareness.

Such integration or assimilation of past experiences into one's construct system can be envisaged as requiring cognitive accommodation in the Piagetian sense (Piaget, 1967). This accommodation usually leads to a tighter (cognitive) understanding of the largely sub-verbal experiences had during cathartic abreaction and should enable the client to put some verbal structure onto these pre-verbal feelings. By learning to put verbal form on feeling, the client is in a better position to discuss his or her experiences with others – including the psychotherapist. This facilitates her adaptation into social structures (Lacan's Social Order). She can also "save" energy heretofore required to repress the memory of those psychodynamically threatening events, with their associated emotions, that were relived during abreaction.

This liberation from a need to repress the past is coupled with increased insight and is associated with an enhanced observer status in everyday life, as one learns to carry over enhanced insight and awareness into one's daily activities. This process, as already mentioned, is assisted by the practice of meditation – non-dual in aspiration.

20   Non-Dual States

As thinking tends to be dualistic, one can say that both the pre-verbal construing of infants and the post-verbal "no-thought" state of advanced meditation are both characterised by degrees of non-dual sense-making. In other words, dualistic construing is largely confined to a band between pre-verbal and post-verbal (or trans-verbal) construing. However, pre-verbal states can be irrational and without access to the higher cognitive functions as found in symbolisation or in transcendence.

Wilber (1996) warned against the "pre/trans fallacy" where infantile pre-verbal states, or pathological regression to such states, are confused with trans-verbal states because both are largely non-verbal. With trans-verbal non-dualistic states all "lower" states remain available for usage, whereas with pre-verbal non-dualistic states this range is not necessarily the case, in that infants and pathologically regressed people do not usually have access to normal or to higher cognitive functions, or to trans-verbal states as found in advanced meditation.

The "no-thought" of deep meditation is similar to the Buddhist doctrine of "emptiness" (Mendoza, 2010). This is a special emptiness or fallow state full of potential in the Taoist sense – ready to give birth to something new. This dynamic, fertile void can be envisaged as the non-dualistic essence out of which all form and performance emerges – including our dualistic thinking. In a parallel way, our universe supposedly emerged from "nothing" with the Big Bang 13.7 billion years ago (Matthews, 2005; DelMonte, 2011a).

Behind all form there is an ultimate unknowable reality called "O" by Bion (1970). Bion also described this as the "absolute truth", the "infinite", the "godhead" and "the thing-in-itself" (Bion, 1970, ch.3, p.26). It is also characterised by formlessness, timelessness and dimensionlessness. According to Bion, knowledge emerges out of this absolute truth through transformation of "O" by the "alpha process", that is by secondary process thinking in the Freudian sense. But, whereas infinite "O" can transform into particular bits of locally held knowledge, the reverse does not apply, as Bion does not accept that bits of knowledge can transform into "O". In other words, whereas the laws of physics and mathematical truths of the Infinite can inform us, we cannot know or influence the Infinite.

The Buddhist viewpoint is that it is possible to transcend the delusion of our self-invented dualistic world, and, in seeing the transparency of our construct system, experience a greater sense of unity with our universe (with "O"?). Such a transformative experience comes from an awareness of how we subjectively and collectively construct our views of this greater reality. This awareness may be unfolded through mindfulness meditation practice. As already mentioned, an aim of this practice is to put us in touch with the inter-penetration and the inter-dependence of all forms of life ("inter-being") and also with compassion (Thich Nhat Hanh, 1975, 1991, 2003). However, things may not always unfold so smoothly.

21   Critique and Conclusions

Compared with psychoanalysts, most teachers of meditation have little to say about finding, accepting and coming to terms with our inner "badness" or destructiveness (such as anger, hatred, lust, envy and the like). Zen Buddhists refer to "*Makyo*" as morbid, unwanted, unconscious material which interferes with meditation by arising spontaneously during its practice (Russell, 1986). Meditation instructors usually do not seek to analyse emergent Makyo or their past causes.

In this respect, the practice of traditional meditation differs from psychotherapy. With the latter, there is an attempt to integrate split-off goodness (ego-ideals and idealised objects) as well as "badness" (our "shadows"), rather than just "side-stepping" our unwanted parts as in meditation (Main, 1982, 1984, 1989; DelMonte 1995a, 1995b, 2004). Psychoanalysts see splitting as weakening the ego. The approach in meditation is to move beyond the dictate of the ego. A difficulty with this approach could be that individuals who have rather fragmented ego identities tend to be drawn to meditation, yet may experience considerable difficulty in transcending their unintegrated egos (DelMonte, 1990).

Paradoxically, we need reasonably good "ego-strength" to help us transcend those ego strivings that temporarily yield some pleasure but ultimately little happiness. To quote Buddhist psychotherapist Jack Engler: "You have to be somebody before you can be nobody" (Wilbur, Engler and Browne, 1991). Hence such transcendence depends for its success on a healthy ego to be able to temporarily suspend its cognitive (i.e. dualistic) functioning (DelMonte, 1987, 1990, 1995b, 2004).

A problem with those who exclusively advocate the *via negativa* is that they tend to deify the "no-self" or "nothingness" experience. Although such experience can have enormous spiritual value for some it can also be a defensive escape into "narcissistic emptiness" (Epstein, 1990). In other words, there can be confusion between egolessness and self-abnegation. The latter has been described as pathological de-personalisation and de-realisation, which are forms of hysterical dissociation (Castillo, 1990).

Concentrative meditation (Samatha) can be mis-used to deny the importance of the body and aspects of external or social reality, thereby increasing splits such as found in "mind/body" and "person/world" or "subject/object" dualisms. Worse still, there is the risk that the *via negativa* can turn into a painless form of premature self-destruction anticipating death; in other words, working more in the service of Thanatos than of Eros.

Thus concentrative meditation can also be used as a psychological defence (Epstein, 1990) – especially in the short-term when it is used to engage in premature relaxation or escapist dissociation (DelMonte, 1990). There is always the possibility that some people will abuse the practice of Samatha as a means of escaping from interacting with painful aspects of social life. Others may turn to Samatha as a defence by using it to distance themselves from what they regard as unworthy parts of themselves – namely their aggression, sexuality, intellect, envy and so forth. But, as Epstein points out, these functions are still present (only denied). "Such people often find themselves irresistibly attracted to powerful others who come to contain essential ego functions that are otherwise disavowed" (Epstein, 1990, p.78). Hence we find the cult leader phenomenon.

The path of mindfulness should not seek to diminish the embodied self, but rather to accomplish the liberation of self from blind allegiance to id impulses and conditioning, as well as from the impoverishment resulting from our defences. Meditation should allow ego just to be ego – neither permanently subjected to repudiation per *la via negativa* nor indulged with narcissistic grandiosity. The insights gained through psychotherapy show us that Eros cannot stand alone without Thanatos (the Yin/Yang interplay) and that the *via negativa*, without the bridle of logic afforded by the *via positiva*, may be no more than an elaborate defence.

Finally, the conclusions of this Chapter may appear rather paradoxical. Having initially argued for the value of the "talking cure" in dealing with somatoform disorders by learning to put verbal form on elusive feelings, we then go on to deconstruct the notion that such verbalisation be seen as a clinical panacea. Here the value of (silent) concentrative and mindfulness meditation is also acknowledged. There are limits to the "talking cure". Learning to put verbal form on feelings can be developmentally liberating, but can also be defensive – as with intellectualisation, mis-attribution and rationalisation – which serve to contort and reframe the truths of our emotional "underworlds" and spiritual "overworlds".

Hence simplistic notions that mind is superior to body, that "abstract" is better than "concrete" or that one "causes" the other, are just dualistic fallacies! The goal is to reach a dialectical, fluid balance between the intellect and the body (or between the head and the heart), thereby developing a flexible and conscious way of relating to the self and to the world. Beyond both matter and mind, or beyond body and language, lies the non-dualistic ineffable domain beyond symbolisation – namely the stillness and silence of Bion's "O" and Matte Blanco's complete "Symmetry".

The practice of mindfulness allows one to pay attention to feelings. Emotions are the, often sub-conscious, connection between mind and body, as well as the connection between bodies (the social domain), and even between the social and the transpersonal. Thus emotions can play an integrative role, especially when they become conscious as feelings. So we end this Chapter near to where we began, by allusion to that mysterious extra-linguistic realm variously described as "Primary Reality" (Kelly), the "Real" (Lacan), complete "Symmetry" (Matte Blanco) or "O"- the "Absolute Truth" (Bion) – so diffuse, and yet so intriguing to many of us.

CHAPTER 3

Consciousness and Mindfulness

1 Introduction

Chapter Three of this book examines the role of enhancing awareness, via the practices of Eastern mindfulness and Western insight psychotherapies, in dealing with the human quest for meaning and in alleviating suffering. Our incessant clinging attachments, rigid identifications, experiential avoidance, somatisation and other obstacles to conscious symbolisation, are examined. This is approached from various Western psychodynamic and existential perspectives, inspired by the writings of Freud, Jung, Bion, Matte Blanco, Assagioli and Perls, among others, as well as from Eastern wisdom tradition perspectives such as Buddhism and Taoism. Potential pitfalls on the path of consciousness enhancement are also discussed.

> For there is nothing either good or bad, but thinking makes it so
> WILLIAM SHAKESPEARE, *Hamlet*, Act 2, Scene 2, Line 267

In our contemporary 21st century world, we are swamped with information from books, magazines, radios, televisions, newspapers, billboards, smart phones and computers. With the advent of the Internet, this is now the age of hyper-communication – in terms of both sheer quantity and speed. If one takes a complete break from one's office for a couple of weeks, then the e-mails, text messages, letters, faxes, phone messages, etc, keep on piling up and await us in intimidating bulk, all demanding instant attention upon our return.

Then there is the endless chatter. Is it any wonder that we compulsively prattle so much? Our minds are probably over-stimulated with a constant barrage of information, on a level unimagined by our ancestors. Our over-talkative mouths reflect, of course, our unstoppable minds: minds which find it increasingly difficult to switch off, as we obsessively talk to ourselves and others. Even when we go on holidays, we take these over-stimulated, hyper-active minds along with us, in frenetic attempts to "enjoy ourselves" via novel forms of stimulation (de Botton, 2003). Well, not quite always – if we learn how. Never before has quiet meditation been more appropriate as an antidote to this volume of mental overdrive. A real mental vacation means just that – a vacant mind. Meditation – whether by means of concentration on only just one stimulus at the time, or temporarily (trying) to remain mindful, i.e. practising being a neutral, non-judgemental observer – aims at minimising the thinking/analytical mind and instead, fostering clearer sensory and reflective awareness. Paradoxically, deep mindfulness, if practised competently, can eventually lead to the experience of a peaceful void or "mindlessness" – characterised by a state of "no thought" – even if it is only for brief moments initially.

In this Chapter of the book the role of enhancing awareness, via the practice of mindfulness, is examined. Mindfulness is viewed as an effective approach in dealing with suffering as caused by our clinging attachments, rigid identifications, experiential avoidance and defensive repression. This is approached from various psychodynamic and existential perspectives inspired by Freud, Jung, Assagioli and Perls, among others. Potential pitfalls on the path of awareness are also discussed. Chapter Three also examines the role of consciousness in well-being from both Eastern and Western perspectives. The practice of mindfulness, like psychoanalysis, offers a non-directive challenge to those psychological defences which tend to distort or reduce our conscious experience of life.

Western psychotherapy praxis has typically been characterised by confidence in the ability of the logical, analytical and thinking mind to resolve most forms of psychological distress, e.g. from the use of Freud's "talking cure" to cognitive therapy's prescriptive dialogues. However, there may be times when very much older Eastern approaches to resolving human suffering are also useful, for example, by the fostering of reflective silence as in meditative practice, with its emphasis on the intuition emergent from the resultant "no thought" state, as well as from mindfulness practice by our embodied minds in the here and now.

The ancient Eastern wisdom traditions, such as Hinduism (for example, Vedic Philosophy as expounded in the Upanishads), Taoism, Sufism and Buddhism, tend to see the verbally labelling, reactive, splitting, grasping or rejecting mind itself as the main obstacle to be overcome. Their practitioners employ a variety of practices such as Koans, promotion of mindfulness, non-attachment, compassion and various meditation and yoga exercises in order to transform and transcend common sources of suffering, such as found in anxiety and depression.

Some of us form rigid emotional attachments to people, material objects, social roles and ideologies. We may also idealise and over-identify with these attachments. Self-reflection, as fostered by depth psychotherapies, mindfulness meditation and the like, may enhance our awareness of these cravings. This in turn may enable us to dis-identify from dysfunctional ideas, habits,

longings and attitudes. We can begin to let go gently of attachments and identifications which no longer constructively serve us on our evolving journeys
through life.

However, extreme detachment may be engaged in defensively by some
people via exaggerated introspective meditation and self-reflection, thus increasing social isolation. Moreover, such escapist introspection may, with
some, lead to split-off self-engrossment rather than to genuine self (and social)
awareness – with its concomitant nurturing and relational engagement.

2   Suffering

Suffering exists in many forms – including our racing, scattered, distracted and
disconnected "jumping-monkey" minds. Rumination is often a factor in the
onset of depression as well as in relapse into depression (Michalak, et al., 2011).
The inability to cognitively inhibit rumination is a major vulnerability factor in
recurrent depression (Ardal and Hammar, 2011).

There are two opposite attitudes towards suffering – namely stoicism and
reformism (Ferry, 2006). The latter is about changing the external world with
political reformation, social change, revolution and the like. The emphasis
here is more on external struggle, so as to change how things were done polit-
ically in the past so as to forge a better social future. From a Taoist perspective
the focus with reformism is on "doing", as in moving a "boulder" if it stands in
our way.

Stoicism, on the other hand, is more concerned with (non-submissive) acceptance, "being" and inward change in the present; flowing (Taoistically) like
water around, under or over the "boulder". Stoicism is normally associated with
such ancient Greeks as the Spartans, but it can be argued that the philosophical stance of stoicism equally applies to Buddhism (Ferry, 2006) and by extension to aspects of other ancient Oriental philosophies such as Taoism and
to some forms of ancient Indian philosophy. Even the writings of early Judeo-
Christianity, based in the Middle East, reveal clear stoic admonitions, e.g. Jesus
of Nazareth's advice to "turn the other cheek" when aggressed. What these stoic philosophies have in common is a focus on *inner* spiritual evolution, rather
than on *external* socio-political "revolution".

The Taoist concept of a flowing balance between the Yin and Yang tendencies within us (and within society) is pertinent here. For example, we need a
balance between personal stoicism and social reformism. Yin and Yang represent a dance between opposing dualistic tendencies within an overall ultimate
unity as symbolised by the Yin-Yang circle, with its wavering line separating
Yin from Yang – yet with Yin containing some Yang potential and vice versa.

For Buddhists, change initially starts with oneself, rather than demanding that others or that society changes. Likewise, for Buddhists, if one must criticise (which is often just a form of projection), then be prepared to look more closely at oneself rather than criticising others (Thich Nhat Hanh, 1975, 1991, 2003). "Radical acceptance" of the "suchness" of external reality is a central feature of Buddhist mindfulness (Hayes and Smith, 2005), as is "being" and consciousness. Radical acceptance is an active stance to life as we encounter it – to be contrasted with passive submission to it. Such stoic "being" can be contrasted with the "doing" mode, that is, with the performance orientation of reformism and its associated focus on (external) form and appearance in the Kantian sense.

Eastern approaches to well-being promote the development of our intuitive and reflective selves in order to deal stoically with suffering, which is often linked to instinctive drives and to conditioned, habitual aspects of mind. In the Judeo-Christian tradition, being born with "original sin" can be seen metaphorically as being born into ignorance, lacking wisdom and being dominated by instincts and conditioned reflexes. Some types of Western psychotherapy, especially psychoanalysis and Gestalt therapy, share aspects of stoicism with Eastern approaches, in so far as the focus is on personal responsibility by developing insight into, or awareness of, the unfree nature of our unexamined minds. For example, Moncayo (2003) sees Lacanian psychoanalysis as operating within the spirit of stoicism. With both mindfulness practice and the "depth" psychotherapies, awareness is typically facilitated by "deep" observation and reflection on oneself and on others.

3   The Talking Cure

So what can we do with anxiously driven and readily distractible minds? Typically, one option is to offer them the "talking therapies" with a "talking cure" in mind! So we have Freud's "free association" monologues, cognitive therapy's "cognitive restructuring" dialogues and many other variants – all using verbalisation as their modus operandi. These are often very useful approaches – usually in the earlier (i.e. "repair") stages of psychotherapy when dealing with deficits, conflicts and defences. But as therapy progresses, alternative approaches may be more effective, for example, with those amongst us with varying degrees of ruminative and obsessive thinking. Can problems of the strained and over-active mind be solved by the *thinking* mind exclusively? Hopefully some clarity on this shall emerge as we proceed.

4   The Inner Observer

One may object that we are also right now engaging in communicative chatter! Well, yes, this has to do with externality. Talking and writing are useful, albeit limited, means of communication between "objects", i.e. between people. Internality, must not, however, be neglected. We are not just objects to each other, we are also subjects. Our internal spaces – our subjectivities – should not be overlooked. Again this is where quiet meditation is also valuable. When we attend to our inner space we often notice how our incessant thinking is like a compulsion, well-nigh impossible to stop, even when we claim that these ruminations are mostly unwanted. This repetitive thinking has typically been dealt with in cognitive therapy by "thought stopping", but evidence suggests that a gentler approach, based on the acceptance of unwanted cognitions via mindful "witnessing", may be more effective (Thich Nhat Hanh, 1975, 1991, 2003; Tolle, 1999, 2005; Barnes-Holmes et al., 2004). This is not a defeatist acceptance, but rather a mindful choice (Hayes and Smith, 2005). There are echoes here of Viktor Frankl's (1967) "paradoxical intention", which encourages one to embrace the feared situation rather than to avoid it.

"Awakening" our "observer" capacity in the here and now is what mindfulness meditation promotes. Much of our private thinking is comprised of unproductive monologues at best (often telling ourselves illusory stories), but also by destructive imaginary, internal disputes and conflicts. Many people suffer from minds which are ceaselessly engaged in anxious or depressive self-statements, in weary "battles" and the like, with little in the way of creative outcome. Many of us "live in our heads" excessively, i.e., in Lacan's (1966) "Imaginary" domain, often experientially disconnected from the reality our bodies and from aspects of society. What can be done about all of this? Well, one can begin to raise one's awareness level by mindfulness training.

5   The Role of Meditation

One should, perhaps, commence practice with a word of caution. For individuals with poor ego-strength it is usually better to engage in reparative psychotherapy prior to taking up meditation (DelMonte, 1990, 2003). Meditation is more about "fine-tuning" and growth, rather than about retrospective "repair" as such. Psychotherapy (literally "soul/mind treatment"), on the other hand, concerns making up for serious emotional deficits and resolving psychodynamic conflicts.

One usually commences meditation with training in quiet concentration ("Samatha") before moving on to mindfulness practice ("Vipassana"). In concentration meditation, by focusing exclusively and continuously on one meaningless stimulus (for example a mantra or one's breath), contrasts tend to fall away. As contrasts are necessary for ordinary sense-making, one is left with little or nothing to construe, i.e. eventually with "no-thought" if adequately adept (DelMonte and Kenny, 1985b; DelMonte, 1987, 2004). This is the nothingness of the *via negativa*. Sustained "nothingness" can lead to an ineffable and non-dualistic mental stance of non-attachment and equanimity, in which one experiences psychological "symmetry", in other words, when typical opposite viewpoints or attitudes (Yin/Yang) appear to be fused, undifferentiated or even identical, which for some is suggestive of Unity or the Absolute (DelMonte, 1995b). Concentrative (Samatha) meditation may thus facilitate the emergence of a "no thought" or fallow state, also referred to as "creative emptiness" by Moncayo (2003).

Having learned to concentrate, it becomes easier to practice mindfulness meditation (Vipassana). Mindfulness meditation has the characteristics of an elevated observer status in the here and now, associated with increased reflexivity, vigilance, circumspection and introspection. Put in sensory processing terms, mindfulness meditation involves increased awareness of our exteroception (via the five senses), of our proprioception (via the muscles and joints), and of our interoception (via the internal organs). In this way relationships may be seen between internal and external events, as well as between one's behaviour, bodily processes and cognition, thereby facilitating integration of the behavioural, emotional, cognitive and social aspects of our experience (DelMonte, 2003, 2004). The enhanced *mindfulness* emergent from Vipassana practice is called "Sati". The *insight* (or enhanced awareness) resulting from Sati is called "Citta". Citta may lead to a form of non-dissociative awareness ("Satipatthana Sutta") where one's consciousness is not split by default, but rather is integrated holistically, for example, by not "living in one's head" – detached from aspects of one's body or from one's physical or social surroundings. This is where the healing ("making whole") takes place. But achieving non-dissociative awareness is not easy, as consciousness is often defensively split, distorted and reduced, thereby affecting our level of awareness.

6   Mindfulness and Dis-Identification

It may be easier to commence mindfulness training by observing our physical bodies in action, for example by watching ourselves just walking as in walking meditation. We can do likewise for various other daily activities, for example, while washing our hands or eating. With the latter, all aspects of eating are observed – biting, chewing, swallowing, etc. This can also be done in groups.

The mindful practice of Hatha Yoga affords us an excellent means to deepen awareness of our dynamic embodiment.

Paradoxically, when we apply our "inner observer" to our own thinking minds while practising mindfulness, it is not just with the intention of "refining" our thinking, but also to learn how to dis-identify from aspects of it (Assagioli, 1965; De Mello, 1990; Holmes, 1997; Tolle, 1999, 2005; DelMonte, 2000b, 2003). Observing the contents of our minds, like clouds passing through the sky without either rejecting or clinging onto them, is what dis-identification (and mindfulness) is basically about. Thereby one learns to let go temporarily of unsolicited and intrusive thoughts so as to have a less "muddied" consciousness, eventually letting go momentarily of all thoughts, rendering moments of clear stillness – or better still, the "just being" of "no thought" or non-dualistic consciousness (DelMonte and Halpin, 2014). Although consciousness with little or no thought is a possibility, its opposite, thought without consciousness is not.

Pure consciousness thus appears to be primary, from which emerges thought as a secondary epi-phenomenon: an epi-phenomenon that can become "parasitic", in the sense that consciousness can play the role of a reluctant host to our unbidden thinking – as in dreams, obsessional ruminations and when "hearing voices" (auditory hallucinations). When, in meditation for example, we experience consciousness without thought, we may be in touch with "just being", i.e. with our non-dualistic deeper essence (beyond mental and physical form). Brain activation produces cognitions and emotions. Quieten this brain activity with focussed meditation and one can be left with moments of "no thought", that is, with clear, unpunctuated and undifferentiated consciousness.

Meditation may thus facilitate the emergence of "creative emptiness" in which deliberate "benevolent depersonalisation" is fostered, characterised by the discarding of unhelpful id impulses and critical super-ego controls (Moncayo, 2003). Meditation may thus be seen as a dynamic process, where the person's own self is that which is being innovatively transformed by using material emergent from the unconscious. Here the unconscious is being viewed in the Jungian sense; that is, as potentially nourishing and adaptive, and not just a reservoir of primitive and disavowed material à la Freud's repressed unconscious.

7 Awareness Training

As already mentioned, the early stages of mindfulness practice can also be seen as a form of sensory awareness training using our executive ego-based "inner observer". Awareness training often starts with self-observation (De Mello,

1990). We have several objects of choice on which to focus our attention, such as our breathing, hearing and so forth. We learn to train, i.e. sensitise, all our senses in this way. This is best done non-analytically and in the "hic et nunc" (here and now) mode. We can also observe our cravings, our dislikes, our clutching and needy minds in action, and by "just letting-be", learn to side–step them. Such stoic side-stepping can be seen as a form of deliberate, adaptive, rather than defensive, dissociation.

Strong identification with the desired contents of one's mind, i.e. with one's attachments, typically leads to fear of their eventual loss and consequently to emotional distress, pessimistic thinking and compensatory behaviour. These cravings can be simply observed, and, for a change, neither judged nor acted upon. We can also become attached to, and identified with, our pain, losses and suffering, as in a felt sense of prolonged victimhood.

So developing an awareness of our varied ego attachments is another aspect of mindfulness training, contradictory as some of these attachments may seem to be. Craving for sensory gratification, for continued existence and for annihilation, corresponding respectively to the Freudian constructs of libido, ego and the death instinct can all be problematic (De Silva, 1990).

Dependence on sensory gratification implies dependence on instinct (id) and on externality. Craving for continued existence (Eros) is a denial of impermanence and of eventual death, while craving for annihilation is a premature surrender to the death wish, i.e. to Thanatos. This can be seen in impulsive aggression turned outwards on others (sadism), or inwards on oneself (masochism), as found with drug and alcohol abuse, self-harm and suicide. Behind the death wish is often a desire to return to a non-suffering peaceful state – free from restless longing, frustration and fear. This peace of mind may be attained while alive, temporarily at least, by meditation, yoga and mindfulness practice, as well as by a range of other cultural, natural and spiritual pursuits.

Many approaches to mental health see the development of self-awareness as beneficial. The insight gained through psychoanalysis is purportedly transmutative in terms of neurotic symptoms (Freud, 1900). Likewise, the self-awareness fostered in Gestalt therapy (Perls, et al., 1973) was seen as therapeutic. Schwartz (1983) saw self-attention *per se* as playing a pivotal homoeostatic, and thus integrative, role. It has also been argued, with some empirical support, that meditation in general, and mindfulness meditation in particular, is conducive to well-being (Shafii, 1973b; Carrington and Ephron, 1975; Deatherage, 1975; Brown and Engler, 1980; DelMonte, 1984a, 1985, 1990; DelMonte and Kenny, 1985b).

Moreover, it has been suggested that increased (non-neurotic) self-awareness, with its attendant clarity of vision, should allow one to make more informed choices, thus enabling one to discard old habits, attitudes and at-tachments that no longer serve our evolving needs. These clinging attachments include, among others, to people, material objects, emotions and ideas. So, is there a link between self-awareness, via self-attention strategies, and health?

8   Attention, Awareness and Self-Regulation

Schwartz's (1983) dysregulation theory can be catch-phrased as: "from repres-sion to disease, versus from mindfulness to health". He postulated that aware-ness promotes health and that repression is associated with "dis-ease". He pro-duced considerable empirical evidence that "repressors" show elevated levels of psycho-physiological distress such as electrocortical (brain-wave), electro-myographical (muscular) and, especially, cardiovascular (heart) arousal. These latter findings are consistent with some later work also showing a significant relationship between defensiveness and haemodynamic (blood pressure) arousal in general and cardiovascular arousal in particular (DelMonte, 1984a, 1985). Repressors also report significantly more physical illness than "true low anxious" subjects (Schwartz, 1983).

Schwartz agrees with Galin (1974) when he proposed that repression is pro-duced by a functional cerebral disconnection syndrome in which the left brain hemisphere (which is usually associated with verbal and analytic functioning) becomes functionally isolated to varying degrees from the right hemisphere, with its relative non-verbal, emotional and spatial function. Schwartz pro-duced evidence that subjects scoring high on repression appear to show more right hemisphere cerebral lateralisation with regard to negative emotions and in situations which are potentially threatening. He also quotes other evidence indicating a relative attenuation of information transfer from the right to the left (more logical) hemisphere in "repressive" compared with "true low anxious subjects". Traumatic memories tend to be stored in the right parietal lobes (van der Kolk and Fisher, 1995). Overall, the right hemisphere seems to be activat-ed in the expression of difficult and disturbing emotions, with the left hemi-sphere being associated with the expression of positive emotions such as joy and happiness.

Two months of mindfulness-based stress reduction training has been shown to lead to a significant shift to a higher ratio of left-sided compared with right-sided brain activation, as well as to a significant increase in anti-body reac-tion to influenza vaccine. Moreover, the magnitude of increase in left-sided activation predicted the magnitude of anti-body titre rise to the vaccination (Davidson et al., 2003). In an interesting review of the literature, various forms of "experiential avoidance", as opposed to "acceptance", were shown to be correlated with a range of symptoms of psychopathology such as panic, anxiety, depression and PTSD (Keogh et al., 2008).

Warrenburg et al, (1981) reported a significantly high proportion of hypertensive individuals being "repressors". For these "hypertensives", the more relaxed they said they were during the speech-task, the higher their blood pressure! This observation is supported by other evidence that high blood pressure (internal arousal or "noise") can be used to dampen cognitive awareness of distress (Dworkin et al., 1979; DelMonte, 1984a).

Schwartz (1983) argued that self-attention, as practised in various mindfulness meditation techniques, "seems to have specific autonomic, self-regulatory, stabilising effects on physiological functioning" (p.114). He contended that self-attention can promote localised healing, "especially if the self-attention is guided by relevant imagery that is targeted to the appropriate part(s) of the body" (p.114). This postulation is interesting in terms of the controversial pioneering work of Meares (1978) in which he used visualisation exercises with cancer patients.

More recent research shows that two months practice of mindfulness-based stress reduction can slow down the progression of HIV by increasing the number of CD4+ T lymphocytes. This improved immune response was dose-related, in that the more mindfulness classes that one attended, the higher the CD4+ T cell levels (Creswell, 2008). This finding is consistent with the previous finding of Davidson et al (2003) reporting an immune response dosage phenomenon in anti-influenza activity associated with mindfulness practice. The above findings provide evidence that mindfulness, i.e. consciousness, can influence the functioning of biological matter and the immune response.

9   Somatisation versus Symbolisation

However, there can be problems in the development of internal representations (and of awareness) and thus of communicative symbolisation. That which cannot be verbally symbolised will instead be acted out, projected or somatised in order to be communicated at a lower level of awareness. We can thus turn to the field of psychosomatic and histrionic disorders where complaints are largely manifested in the somatic format. Patients with psychosomatic symptoms tend to be very concrete in their presentation of complaints due to a difficulty with verbal symbolisation (DelMonte, 2001c).

Such patients often show varying degrees of alexithymia in that they have difficulty identifying and naming their own feelings and those of others

(Vanheule et al., 2011). The word "a-lexi-thymia" hails from ancient Greek and means "without words (for) feelings". Unsurprisingly, this condition invariably leads to inter-personal problems (Vanheule et al., 2010), as not being able to notice, locate, name and communicate feelings in oneself and in others handicaps the social self. It often leads to a range of psychological disorders including depression and eating disorders (Fonagy et al., 2011). Developing one's "theory of mind", i.e., an understanding the dynamic phenomenon of mind in oneself and in others, is important in social intercourse (Fonagy, et al., 1994, 2011). Without an appropriate awareness of the complexity of mind, it is difficult to be empathic. The ability to "read" other people's minds and to know what they are making of your mind, is crucial in forging satisfactory relationships. Such empathy is probably be enhanced by increased mindfulness and awareness.

10   Attachments

Much has been said elsewhere (DelMonte, 2003, 2004) about our clutching minds attaching to our opinions, appearances, possessions, success, power, status, prestige, wealth, pride and so forth. Less has been stated about our minds' equal capacity to identify with, and ruminate on, suffering, by either living in the past in holding onto bygone insults, losses, hurts, defeats, etc, or by anticipating the future in pessimistic, paranoid or hypochondriacal ways. Victimhood can, with some people, become a fixed identity, i.e. an attachment and even a way of life (Tolle, 1999; Bruckner, 2000). The chronic "pain-body" (Tolle, 1999, 2005) and the pain-mind are sometimes characterised by an exaggerated need to linger in and talk about suffering compulsively and self-righteously – usually blaming others for our current misery, not always without justification. Then there is the compulsion to compare and judge others from a "knowing" position. Engaging in such non-compassionate "sitting in judgement" and "forming opinions" self-righteously about others only serves to isolate us. Narcissistic pain is inevitable if one is closely identified with one's egotistic mind, which seeks a constant array of ego gratifications, including the need to be always right or victorious. Ego identifications lead us to cling to past gains, regret past losses and worry about future snags, snares, pitfalls and more losses; thereby taking us away from living more fully in the present – especially when it can have so much to offer. Life inevitably involves a series of gains and losses. Griffin (2001) saw adjustment to loss as a lifelong regenerative learning process. Losses also open up spaces for new opportunities.

Then there is the social domain. Attachment has both physiological and psychological components. Developing a "theory of mind" in childhood facilitates healthy attachments (Fonagy et al, 1994). People often remark on the proclivity of human beings to form strong emotional bonds. We are popularly described as "social animals". However, there is considerable variation in this tendency to seek out others and to maintain contact. Social "stickiness" does not appear to be spread evenly in the population. Some individuals deliberately enhance their out-reaching social skills, whilst others, for a variety of reasons, use various strategies to distance themselves from people or to withdraw into themselves. We shall go on to explore the way Eastern approaches, in particular, can be used to modify these apparently opposite inclinations – to either "connect" with others or to retreat from them.

Much has been written about the manner in which children learn to socialise as they grow up. Establishing "healthy" roles and social links is seen as a prerequisite to mental health. Those of us who are unable to form and sustain intimate affiliations are usually perceived as having serious emotional problems – but so are those whose emotional bonds are overly dependent. In other words, extremes in emotional distance, that is, being either too closely enmeshed in a dependent way or, at the other end of the scale, being excessively self-reliant, are considered socio-maladaptive in adults (see Birchnell, 1997).

As already alluded to, we not only become attached to people, we also form strong attachments (including addictions) to a range of objects and experiences, such as the taste of certain foods and drinks, the sound of particular forms of music, our possessions such as childhood toys, paintings, ornaments, land, houses, money, etc. Moreover, we also become attached to the non-material realm in terms of our languages, religions, ethnic groups, theories, ideologies and achievements. We may identify with such attachments, to the point of describing ourselves in terms of their labels. So we may strongly characterise ourselves as "communist", "nationalist", "feminist", "Protestant", "Orthodox", "liberal", "left-wing", "Afrikaans-speaking", "humanist", etc. We also characterise these attachments in egotistical terms, e.g. my religion, my flock, my people, my career, my territory, in my opinion, and so forth, and express strong dislikes and even outright rejection of other identities. So, is our real identity the sum of such potentially divisive, personal attachments, or is this just our mask hiding a deeper essence? We may cling as arduously onto non-material as onto material attachments, e.g. try persuading an "opinionated" person to change his, or her, mind! Attachments do not always make much rational sense. We can become attached to, or enmeshed with, other people's' difficulties, our own personal problems and abusive relationships. Attachments can limit, hold and constrain consciousness to particular viewpoints, attitudes and perspectives. They can imprison and isolate us, impeding our further development.

11   Attachment and Loss

However, attachment and loss are two sides of the same coin. Nothing is permanent – all is flux. Much is illusion and even delusion. All investments are potential losses – if not during our current lifetimes, then certainly upon their physical ends. We all live in the shadow of death – the ultimate narcissistic blow to which we must surrender! This knowledge – coloured by our own personal history of previous losses (both emotional and material) – has as a consequence that we can feel varying degrees of insecurity about our desired attachments.

Paradoxically, the various objects and people on whom we have become dependent for our emotional identity and security may also become the very source of our deepest anxiety, as observed in the "separation anxiety" linked to their feared loss. Although with emotional attachment comes varying degrees of social support, this support is often at a price – namely that of burdensome counter demands and responsibilities. Caring for others can be emotionally draining – not just rewarding!

12   Defensive Detachment

Some of us try to avoid this anxiety by means of a "schizoid defence". It is likely to be found in those of us who are fearful of the risks involved in emotional inter-dependence, often due to past failures and hurts in this area. This defence is characterised by a contrived emotional detachment (largely unconscious) based on an exaggerated attitude of personal self-sufficiency, often where childhood bonding with care-givers was painfully inadequate or insensitive. In the absence of adequate parental attunement and nurturing behaviour, emotional self-dependency may be sought via varying degrees of emotionally insulating and "autonomous" behaviour. An extreme version of this defence could be the affective "non-attachment" (and non-attunement) found in borderline personality disorder, where long-term intimacy is too uncomfortable or difficult to be sustained (see Holmes, 1997). However, several variants of defensive isolation, or extreme egoism, exist. Solipsism, for example, is an intellectual rationalisation for this cut-off stance in life. But is mere withdrawal adequate?

How can one really enjoy such false "escapism" when surrounded by others who may be in pain? Yes it is also possible to use our "inner observer" in a largely selfish manner. This issue of defensive detachment shall be expanded on later.

13   Adaptive Dis-Identification

Not all forms of detachment are maladaptive defences. As already mentioned, some psychotherapists deliberately encourage a form of non-attachment as a way of coping with potential loss. Both Assagioli (1965) and, later, Holmes (1997) refer to the strategy of "dis-identification" when dealing with psychic pain. Assagioli's "Psychosynthesis" perspective was similar to that of those Buddhists who perceive our tendency to identify in a clinging way to objects of our desire as ultimately leading to the pain of their actual or imagined loss. He described cognitive exercises to encourage the development of a mental set of "dis-identification" as a counter-force in coping with this tendency to over-invest and to over-identify ourselves with our physical bodies, emotions, thoughts, etc., and with our attachments in general. The objective of Assagioli's "dis-identification" exercises is to be less at the mercy of our longings, wishes and desires. One finds an echo here of the Buddhist dictum that craving is a source of suffering. Mindfulness training can raise awareness of our acquisatorial nature and help liberate us from the slavery of endless hedonistic grasping, of which contemporary materialism and consumerism are obvious examples. For Freud (1900, 1912, 1930) the pull of the pleasure principle is not freedom: it represents only one side of a dualism, the other side being the reality principle and the displeasure which often follows in the heels of pleasure satiation. Psychological freedom also comes from letting go of defensive and reactionary views and from moving beyond polarised construing as in "them versus us" attitudes.

Let us now look at a non-clinical example of dis-identification. The exile, or migrant, is an interesting case, especially if he, or she, comes from a poorly understood cultural background or ethnic group. Being a migrant in a foreign land often means that one's former cultural identity has to be suspended while a new one is being constructed. Todorov (1996) refers to the latter process as acculturation. Here we should also speak of de-constructing one's former persona (or de-culturisation) and developing a new identity (or mask?). This can be a painful process, characterised by considerable nostalgia for lost familiarities and by obsessional reminiscing about the lost world, in an attempt to keep it mentally alive while we construct a new one. But this process is rarely fully complete, so that one is left as a transcultural hybrid, betwixt two worlds. Rather than view this new state of affairs as a failure, it could, on the contrary, be seen as an adaptive dynamic in which one's identity is "elastic". Fixity gives way to resilient flexibility in which acquisitions (identifications) are constantly being balanced by losses (dis-identifications) to produce a freshly evolving self. But nothing of real value needs to be really lost – even if external circumstances appear to impose this. One may be forced to relinquish external attachments (e.g. through bereavement), but these external losses (e.g. loved ones) can instead be internalised and carried around in us symbolically so as to enrich our lives. In this way we abandon nothing that we still value as it becomes part of us (Hillesum, 1986).

14   Non-Attachment Techniques of the Orient

As already alluded to, in the Orient there is a long tradition, going back thousands of years linked to Hinduism, Taoism and Buddhism, of using various techniques such as meditation, Yoga, Tai-chi, Qi-gong and so forth to achieve non-dualistic mental states characterised by equanimity and non-grasping, by moving beyond (i.e. "transcending") the issues and problems onto which our dualistic ("me versus other") thoughts can "stick" (see Mascaro, 1962; DelMonte, 1995a; DelMonte, 2000b). Meditation, Hatha Yoga, and Qi-gong exercises can be used to focus on bodily posture, balance, breathing and the contents of one's mind. Also the Tao concept of a flowing balance between Yin and Yang tendencies within us (and within society) is pertinent. For example, we need a balance between personal stoicism and social reformism. Yin and Yang represent the dance between dualistic tendencies within an overall ultimate unity as symbolised by the Yin-Yang circle.

   All the above (like the use of Zen Koans) play down the value of intellectualisation, rationalisation and other aspects of what is known as "shi-shen" in ancient Chinese Qi-gong. Shi-shen, or conceptual knowledge, must be balanced by "yuan-shen" which lies beyond conceptual consciousness, yet permeates all aspects of life – being its very source. Yuan-shen is seen as the dynamic force inherent in "Qi". Qi could be referred to as "vital energy" in the West. Yuan-shen, being essentially non-dualistic and ineffable, is difficult to symbolise verbally. During meditation and Koan contemplation one tries to side-step the dualistic discursive mind with its focus on conceptual knowledge or shi-shen. The periods of meditative "no thought" characterised by stillness, silence and openness may present opportunities to experience the ineffable yuan-shen referred to above. Moreover, yuan-shen may be phenomenologically similar to

Jung's (1958) "collective unconscious", namely to a vast, loose, pre-verbal, pre-conscious, non-dualistic and inchoate transpersonal resource of vast potential. This resource can be "tapped into" more readily by the use of certain techniques such as meditation in which the chattering conceptual mind is temporarily silenced. Lose thy mind and come to thy senses – in the here and now!

A distinction can usefully be made between ego "detachment", which implies detaching, i.e. withdrawing interest or giving up something previously valued on the one hand, and "non-attachment" on the other, which implies a more neutral witnessing and non-grasping stance whilst accepting, in a non-possessive manner, all of that which momentarily forms part of our experiential world. Whereas detachment can seem anti-social, non-attachment does not imply a lack of compassion, nor indifference to the world or to the lot of others. Detachment can also be seen as harbouring strong defensive undertones and may have little to do with maturing through life's experiences – be they work or love related.

15   More Advanced Mindfulness Meditation Practice

Advanced practitioners of meditation often focus their attention on the phenomenology of consciousness itself by means of introspective mindfulness (DelMonte, 1995a; Kabat-Zinn, 1996, 2005). With mindfulness techniques the meditator is encouraged to maintain "a quiet awareness, without comment, of whatever happens to be here and now" (Watts, 1957). This aspect of mindfulness is characterised by calm awareness and presence. Another aspect of mindfulness is a curious, investigative attitude. An objective of mindfulness meditation is "to come to know one's own mental processes, to thus begin to have the power to shape or control the mental processes, and finally to gain freedom from the condition where the mental processes are unknown and uncontrolled, with the individual at the mercy of his own unbridled mind" (Deatherage, 1975, p.134).

Hendricks (1975) sees such introspection as a form of discrimination training, helping meditators to observe their own thoughts in a relatively neutral way. He speculates that "since nearly everyone has a certain number of neurotic thoughts, mental health is dependent upon the ability to recognise that they are "just thoughts"" (p.145). This approach can be applied to depressive, anxious and obsessive cognitions and several authors have done just that (e.g. Kabat-Zinn, 1996, 2005; Teasdale, 2000).

A variant of meditational mindfulness (analytic mindfulness meditation) can also used to observe the phenomenology of felt attachments, with their complex interwoven webs of emotional, cognitive, attitudinal and behavioural sub-components (DelMonte, 2003). In observing the construction of consciousness from these components in a non-attached (i.e. non-grasping or non-identificatory manner) practitioners hope, at least temporarily, to move beyond the pull of their unbridled "ego" yearnings and the push of irrational dislikes. Being mindful of the impermanence of all material and psychic attachments facilitates awareness of the ephemeral nature of our personal consciousness, laden as it is with regular eruption of instinctive craving. Freedom is where craving is converted into mindful choice. If cravings are invariably suppressed then we are no freer than if we always yield to them! Acceptance of "the now", by neither clinging to nor rejecting our experiences, is the essence of mindfulness (and of new learning). Its aim is to free us from our reactionary minds, i.e. minds dominated by instinct and by past conditioning.

Advanced mindfulness meditation encourages an opening to broader consciousness, i.e., to "egoless" observing or "just witnessing". One can say that such practice favours an opening of our intuitive self. It fosters this intuitive self over our more driven instinctive self and reactive conditioned self, as well as over our "split-off" cerebral self. The insights gleaned from advanced meditation are not to be limited to personal gain, but are preferably transformed into relational acts of kindness, compassion, respect and tolerance of others. Acceptance of the suchness of reality does not preclude compassionate work towards improving the lot of ourselves and that of others, but rather sets it on a sounder footing.

16   The Silence of Meditation

Meditation, with practice, can become very simple. For example, we can learn to observe the silence and unity consciousness within us – if we progress that far. One's relationship to space and time may take on new perspectives. Moments of apparent timelessness may emerge, as may a sense of formlessness. Our personal experience of timelessness is just a small chip off the eternity "block", and our experience of formlessness yields a sense of spatial infinity. These non-dualistic moments of dwelling in spatial infinity, timelessness and formlessness, however brief they may be, nevertheless yield a sense of unity where the personal, dualistic and discursive mind has suspended its typical "me/other" asymmetrical construing. By letting go of dualistic sense-making and just "letting be", one approaches whatever emerges with increasing equanimity. Deeply silent meditation, characterised by "egoless" observing, "no thought", and by a sense of unity, brings us in touch with yet-to-be expressed

potential – a real break from predictable and repetitive thinking. This experience resonates with the Dutch 17th century pantheist and monist philosophy
of Baruch de Spinoza, who argued that matter and mind are differentiated attributes of the one and same substance – namely that of (non-dual) "Nature/
God" (Guenancia, 2009).

All theoretical concepts are merely words pointing to bodily, psychological
and social experiences. Such verbal labels often fail to do justice to actual experience. Moreover, the dichotomy between the discursive mind and no-thought
does not imply an inherent conflict. Rational thinking undoubtedly has its value
and place – especially when we use thought and speech to facilitate informative,
creative, humorous or playful communication. Silence, on the contrary, facilitates communion (Shafii, 1973a), i.e. the meeting of minds (or rather of "hearts")
non-verbally through intuition, feeling, empathy and sensation. This can thus be
an intimate silence. Words can lead to emotional distance – not just closeness.

As Jung (1971a) pointed out there are four ways of knowing – i.e., thinking,
sensation, feeling and intuition – with thinking being increasingly favoured
in contemporary Western education. However, with the silence of meditation,
one initially uses focussed sensory attention (sensation) in order to quieten
the mind and foster the emergence of intuitive knowing.

The practice of silent meditation leading to "no thought" can be described
as the *via negativa* (the empty way) as opposed to the *via positiva*, which is
the more habitual mode as seen daily in our discursive minds. They represent
opposite (yet equally valid) ways of sense making. The path of meditation (silence) should not seek to negate the mind in action, but rather to assist in
the liberation of one's self from blind allegiance to our instinctual impulses,
obsessions and compulsions (Freud's id), and also assist us from fleeing from
our dislikes and fears. It may also free us from the impoverishment resulting
from our maladaptive defences, which primarily serve to limit our awareness,
and from judgemental attitudes (Freud's "harsh" super-ego). As already mentioned, silence and mindful meditation thus facilitate the emergence of "creative emptiness" in which "benevolent depersonalisation" is fostered (Moncayo,
2003). This is a clearer type of consciousness – less muddied by conditioned
and instinctive eruptions.

17   Mindfulness in Psychodynamic Psychotherapy

Western insight psychotherapy, compared with Eastern mindfulness meditation, is a neophyte on the world stage. Both, nevertheless, are concerned with
enhancing awareness. The insight sought from the depth psychotherapies

and the *citta* emergent from mindfulness meditation may, in some respects, be similar. Both approaches, in the long-term, show us how to observe, analyse and understand ourselves and others, i.e., how to become personally and socially more reflective. Both approaches are thus concerned with enhanced knowledge, but not necessarily just with intellectual insight.

Melanie Klein (1928) ventured so far as to postulate the existence of an "epistemophilic instinct" as a kind of curiosity or motivational force driving one towards discovery. However, Bion (1970, 1974) took her view further by arguing that the quest for knowledge is not always evident in people. In fact, its opposite is also found. For Bion, the defensive denial of reality is one pole of a dialectic whose opposite pole is mental growth through knowledge, which may involve *working through* psychic pain. "The more a person is inclined towards evacuating pain, the more he denies reality and the less he is capable of mental growth" (Pelled, 2007, p.1520). Here Pelled sees and advocates a clear correspondence between Buddhism and psychoanalysis.

Both of the above approaches "practice what they preach" in that one cannot either teach mindfulness or conduct psychoanalysis without first subjecting oneself to the same discipline. However, unlike meditation, most forms of psychotherapy use verbalisation as their *modus operandi*. A common view held by psychoanalysts is that those who do not learn to "think through" (i.e. to symbolise verbally) are bound to "act out" and to continue suffering – as with the hysterically inclined who tend to "feel" too much (DelMonte, 1991). Hence we have the "pain-body" (Tolle, 1999), a somatising body impoverished in terms of its capacity for reflective thinking.

Whilst one would not dispute that there is great merit in the "talking cure" approach there is, nevertheless, a growing corpus of opinion on the value of some fecund silence in therapy. For example, the obsessionally inclined, in thinking and often talking compulsively, tend to block out feelings and demonstrate that we cannot always just "think" our way of out of problems. In psychotherapy they typically have difficulty in being "in touch" with feelings – their own and those of others – and are usually very uncomfortable with silence. Hence the endless chatter, which is often split off from feeling. This was pejoratively referred to as "free disassociation" (Perls, et al., 1973) or split-off intellect. These people may need to learn that speech, just like music, is given deeper meaning by being punctuated by fertile silence, so that something more profound than more words may emerge.

Jung's (1958a) concept of *coniunctio* (or the marriage of opposites) is relevant here. For example, love versus hatred, masculine versus feminine, compulsive speech versus frozen silence, as well as conscious versus unconscious, are examples of dynamic opposites which, by means of Jung's "transcendent function", can interact to create a new insightful psychic product (Jung, 1958a, p.90; Bravesmith, 2012). This is similar to a thesis and an anti-thesis producing a creative, over-arching synthesis in Hegelian dialectics. It appears that both Jung's "transcendent function" and Hegel's dialectics are consistent with Heraclitus's "Harmony of Opposites", which postulates an underlying unity between opposing tendencies.

Outer busyness can also be contrasted with inner stillness. According to O'Donoghue (1977, p.133) "If you are outside of yourself, always reaching beyond yourself, you avoid the call of your own mystery. When you acknowledge the integrity of your solitude, and settle into its mystery, your relationships with others take on a new warmth, adventure and wonder". Silence can also be used to foster a sense of compassionate communion in psychoanalysis, complementing the communication wrought by words.

However, silence on the part of the patient was seen as resistance by Freud (1912). But Balint (1958, p.338) argued that "if we can change our own approach – from considering silence as a symptom of resistance to studying it as a possible *source of information* – then we may learn something about this area of mind". Later authors saw silence as indicative of shyness, shame, sorrow, anger, hostility, psychic absence and fear (Shafii, 1973a; Coltart, 1992). Silence has also, at times, been construed, as adaptive regression to pre-verbal sense-making, as opposed to malign or psychotic regression (Shafii, 1973a).

The psychoanalyst Coltart (1992) went as far as saying that "my own preference above all others, is for a silent patient". This may be because the relatively silent patient (and analyst) allows the analyst ample time to identify and work with the visceral felt-sense of the counter-transference. It should come as no surprise that Coltart also described herself as a practitioner of meditation and Buddhism. This is a long way from Freud, who typically did not work with the counter-transference. He saw religious experience, meditation and mysticism as regressive, irrational and maladaptive phenomena, i.e. forms of "oceanic" fusion and oneness with mother, or the wish to re-experience intra-uterine life (Freud, 1930). To facilitate the patient in adaptive regression, i.e. in attenuating her defences, the therapist must also be capable of silence, e.g. by avoiding premature, aggressive and excessive interpretations, instructions or comments. In this way, the patient's pre-verbal traumata can be "re-experienced and mastered again in silence" (Shafii, 1973a, p.442). The patient can then proceed one step further and verbally label any emergent feelings, thereby facilitating communicative symbolisation – in psychotherapy and beyond.

Dreams also tend to be silent. It is well known that Freud (1900) described dreams as the "royal road to the unconscious". Perhaps less well known is that Jung (1958) similarly described meditation as a "sort of a royal road to the unconscious" (p.508). Jung, however, also saw meditation as a "surrender" to the collective unconscious, as its practice leads primarily to an indefinite experience of oneness and timelessness, which according to Jung are hallmarks of the collective unconscious. An encounter with the collective unconscious could be an overwhelming experience for those with poor ego strength. Kretschmer (1962) also saw meditation in a similar light: "Dreams are similar to meditation except meditation gains the reaction of the unconscious by a technique which is faster than depending on dreams" (Kretschmer, p.76). What emerges during the early stages of meditation practice is more likely to be abreactive ("unstressing") rather than equanimous and peaceful "no thought".

By now it should be obvious that it is not just meditators who strive to clear the mind of its sticky attachments. Psychoanalysts like Bion (1970), Shafii (1973a), Khan (1977) and Coltart (1992) also saw value in analysts themselves temporarily creating an empty or "fallow" state of mind during clinical sessions so as to be more receptive to the patient's transferences (DelMonte, 1995b). Bion (1970) advised therapists to forsake memory, desire and understanding during clinical practice. He quoted from a letter written by the English poet John Keats in 1817 in which Keats referred to "negative capability" as "when a man is capable of being in uncertainties, mysteries, doubts, without any irritable reaching after fact and reason" (Bion, 1970, p.125). Here we see a psychoanalyst advising his colleagues not to hold too tightly onto one's professional opinions and theories when dealing with an individual patient, because for Bion (1974) there are other ways of knowing, including the religious and the artistic. These alternative modes require an opening up to aesthetic emotion – which, unlike an anaesthetised emotionally cut off state, enhances awareness of sensation, intuition and feelings of unity (Reid, 1990).

The silent mindfulness emergent from meditation training allows the analyst to listen more deeply to his or her patients, to receive and register their projections, and to let go of these projections after the therapy session. Several psychoanalysts (e.g. Speeth, 1982; Rubin, 1985) see the practice of meditation as enhancing psychoanalytic attention and listening. These claims are consistent with the research finding that patients do better with psychotherapists who practice mindfulness (Crepmair et al., 2007). So, let us take a closer look at this relationship.

18   Psychoanalysis as Mindfulness

An important aspect of advanced mindfulness practice is "choiceless awareness" (Krishnamurti, 1991), i.e. paying attention to *all* which enters

consciousness without selection or censorship, or if one prefers, without clinging or rejection. Another related aspect of mindfulness is "bare witnessing",
i.e. perceiving without judgement, opinion and similar ego strivings. These are
both components of the "de-automatisation" of consciousness, that is, the suspension of habitual sense making.

Both "choiceless awareness" and "bare witnessing" are rather similar to
Freud's (1990) "basic rule" of free association for patients:

"For the purpose of self-observation with concentrated attention, it is advantageous that the patient should take up a restful position and close his eyes; he
must be explicitly instructed to renounce all criticism of the thought formations
which he may perceive. He must also be told that the success of the psychoanalysis depends upon his noting and communicating everything that passes through
his mind, and that he must not allow himself to suppress one idea because it
seems to him unimportant or irrelevant to the subject, or another because it
seems nonsensical. He must preserve an absolute impartiality in respect to his
ideas" (Freud, 1900, p.175). This is so difficult to achieve that it can be said that
analysands are well on the way to successful analyses when they manage to free-
ly associate in Freud's terms, i.e. to speak without selection or self-censorship!

However, for psychoanalysts themselves, Freud's instructions on listening to
their patients are also reminiscent of choiceless mindfulness:

> It simply consists in making no effort to concentrate the attention on an-
> ything in particular, and in maintaining in regard to all that one hears the
> same measure of calm, quiet attentiveness of evenly hovering attention
> ... ... For as soon as the attention is deliberately concentrated in a cer-
> tain degree, one begins to select from the material before one; one point
> will be fixed in the mind with particular clearness and some other con-
> sequently disregarded, and in this selection one's expectations and one's
> inclinations will be followed. This is just what must not be done; however,
> if one's expectations are followed in this selection, there is a danger of
> never finding anything but what is already known ...
>
> FREUD, 1912, pp. 111–112

Hence, from a mindfulness viewpoint, both the analysand and the analyst are
expected to engage in mindful, choiceless awareness, in which neither party
should select, censor, criticise or pursue particular avenues. Moreover, Freud's
advice to the analyst to employ "evenly hovering attention" between patient
and self, as if he, or she, had a floating "third eye" adds an extra layer of reflection to the art of deep listening, namely by encouraging the analyst to observe
oneself, observing one's analysand.

Heimann (1960) also raised the issue of counter-transference by exhorting analysts to *sustain* their affective states during analysis. "What distinguishes this relationship from others is not the presence of feelings in one partner, the patient, and their absence in the other, the analyst, but the *degree* of feeling the analyst experiences and the use he makes of these feelings. ... (and his ability). ... to *sustain* his feelings as opposed to discharging them like the patient" (p.152). Such an approach by the analyst is akin to the deep non-reactive observing which characterises mindfulness.

We have drawn attention above to a certain overlap between "depth" psychotherapy (especially psychoanalysis) and the practice of mindfulness meditation by referring to the ideas of Freud, Jung, Klein, Bion, Coltart, Shafii, Balint, Khan, Speeth, Rubin and Kretschmer. But no list would be complete without briefly referring to the work on the "Bi-logic" of symmetry versus asymmetry by the Chilean psychoanalyst Ignacio Matte Blanco (1988). Matte Blanco described five levels of construing, from the highly, "asymmetrical", i.e. differentiated, discriminatory, logical and tight thinking associated with the distinctions of science and mathematics at one end of a spectrum, to the total "symmetry" (no differences) of the unconscious at the other end. As one moves from tight, conscious Aristotelian logic, characteristic of the sciences and mathematics, towards the deeper layers of the unconscious, there is an increase in looseness, in vagueness, in metaphor, in poetic licence, in symmetry and in fusion, coupled with a decrease in clear-cut identities as differences become blurred (e.g. between internal and external; mother and wife). Bion's (1970, 1974) concept of maternal "reverie" with respect to the mother/infant dyad also comes to mind here in terms of its fusion, communion and looseness of construing. Increasing symmetry (linked to decreasing logical consciousness) gradually abolishes awareness of time and space, so that duality also disappears. This can also be achieved by meditation when one arrives at the "no thought" state. However, for individuals with poor ego strength, increasing symmetry and fusion can lead to confusion and even to florid psychosis.

Besides psychoanalysis, other forms of psychotherapy, in particular Gestalt Therapy, also question the value of too much emphasis on intellectualisation in therapy, preferring instead to focus on the enhancement of awareness.

19   Gestalt Therapy Perspective

Fritz Perls, the founder of Gestalt therapy, was influenced by Tao philosophy and Indian Yoga, as well as by Freud, Reich, Mareno, Gestalt psychology and existentialism (Perls et al., 1973). He emphasised personal responsibility in the resolution of problems. Both Gestalt therapy and mindfulness meditation practice focus on the "*hic et nunc*" (here and now) of actual experience. That is, both meditation and the various Gestalt techniques play down the value of abstract verbalisation. In fact, Perls et al. (1973) stated that verbalisation, as in free association, could become a sort of escapist "free-disassociation" from feelings and semi-conscious emotions. Together with obsessional verbalisation, Perls also saw excessive rationalisation as a defence against unprocessed subjective feelings.

Instead, Perls stressed the importance of "contact" and "sensing", hence his admonition to lose thy (thinking) mind and come to thy senses. He described many specific techniques, involving sensation, used to foster awareness. In this regard it is worth noting that Perls, although psychoanalytically trained, defined himself as an existentialist who applied the phenomenological approach (Perls et al, 1973). The phenomenological method used by many existentialists is a means of subjective inquiry originally developed by Edmund Husserl as a way to examine one's immediate experience (DelMonte, 1989a, 1989b). This involves a critical and scrupulous inspection of one's mental processes and of one's consciousness. As existentialist phenomenology concerns subjective awareness without pre-judgement, it could be argued that it closely resembles the technique of mindfulness meditation in that the latter is purportedly characterised by a de-automatisation of experience, i.e. the suspension of perceptual and cognitive habits (DelMonte, 1989a, 1989b). With both the mindfulness and phenomenological methods one strives for a permeable (or open) stance to the flux of consciousness without trying to punctuate any experience had.

In both mindfulness and Gestalt therapy, the observer role is valued. For example, Perls encouraged patients to observe tension and anxiety and not to engage in "premature relaxation", i.e. to sustain attention. In other words, Perls, like Jung (1958, 1958a, 1971a), Heimann (1960) and his fellow existentialist Frankl (1967), as well as Bion (1970, 1974) and Pelled (2007), promoted "approach techniques", i.e., stoicism, rather than avoidance of legitimate discomfort and suffering. In the same way, in mindfulness meditation one is encouraged to observe steadfastly one's moods, feelings, thoughts, and so forth in a non-attached and non-judgemental way, that is neither clinging to them nor pushing them away.

Perls, like Schwartz (1983) and many practitioners of meditation saw awareness *per se* as being therapeutic. This even included awareness of simply "being" for which he used his "internal silence" and "make a void" techniques in order to suspend the dualism within. Perls acknowledged an influence from Taoist philosophy here, and the similarity between Perls's internal silence technique and the "no thought" strategy of concentrative meditation is striking (DelMonte, 1990).

Perls also used breathing exercises similar to those found in breath meditation. Both involve paying deep attention to one's breathing. In Gestalt therapy
there are also exercises for focussing on anxiety, panic, depression, fatigue, psychosomatic symptoms and behavioural problems – all in order to "integrate"
and resolve them, thus leading to Gestalt "closure". Likewise, mindfulness is
increasingly being used with a similar range of psychological disorders (Kabat-
Zinn, 1996, 2005; Teasdale, 2000).

20   Abreaction, Insight and Integration

It has been argued by McGee, et al. (1984) that emotional experiences which
are too threatening to one's core psychological functioning can be defensively suspended as "un-experienced experiences", in other words, without being
fully processed or integrated at a conscious level. This phenomenon has also
already been referred to as "experiential avoidance" and was shown to be correlated with a range of symptoms of psychopathology such as panic, anxiety,
depression and PTSD (Keogh et al., 2008).

In a sense, such "undigested" experiences remain akin to the "unfinished
business", the "unfulfilled needs", or the "incomplete Gestalten" referred to by
Gestalt therapists. These incomplete Gestalten are usually at low levels of cognitive awareness and tend to be psychologically projected or "acted out" behaviourally when trying to achieve emotional closure, or in order to be communicated – often with considerable hysterical feeling but with little reflection.
In this sense the symptoms of hysteria are seen to be functional and symbolic
(Szasz, 1972b; DelMonte, 2001c).

It may be that the weakening and loosening of one's cognitive defences
during Gestalt therapy, free association and meditation facilitates hypnoidal
states and the abreactive emergence of incomplete Gestalten and other repressed or dissociated material (DelMonte, 1981, 1984b). In other words, the
experience which was held in a sort of "suspended animation" can be relived
emotionally – initially as "somatic memory", then with hindsight reprocessed
and integrated at a more insightful level of awareness. Following abreaction,
patients can try to verbally label any pre-verbal emotions that they have just
experienced. By learning to put verbal form on feeling, the patient is in a better position to relate his or her experiences to others – including to the psychotherapist. This liberation from a need to repress the past is coupled with
increased insight. It is associated with an enhanced observer status in everyday life, as one learns to carry over enhanced insight and awareness into one'
daily activities.

21   Potential Problems with Detachment and Dis-Identification

As mentioned earlier, there are individuals whose attachments are problematic, being either too intense or overly dependent, or in the other direction, practically non-existent. Does meditation ever encourage an exaggerated introverted stance to the external world, at times bordering on pathological dissociation and fostering social isolation, i.e. the avoidance, or even rejection, of the relational domain?

Epstein (1990) thought that meditation could lead to "narcissistic emptiness" as ego-strivings aimed at the external world are negated. Castillo (1990), in a similar vein, could see excessive meditation practice as leading to pathological de-realisation and de-personalisation, as both the external world and the self are eschewed. These comments shall be returned to later.

Those forms of meditation which employ a relaxed posture, closed eyes and the rhythmical and monotonous repetition of a mantra, encourage a shift away from one's habitual construing of external reality towards a trance-like state in which suggestibility may be enhanced (DelMonte, 1981; 1984b). Thus mantra meditation, like hypnotic induction, can weaken one's ability to marshal one's cognitive defences, thereby encouraging partial dissociation between external reality and one's inner world dominated by memories, fantasies, wishes, desires, and the like. It has also been argued that turning attention away from the external world facilitates an exploration of the internal realm, including the unconscious and archetypal imagery in the Jungian sense (see DelMonte, 1995a, 1995b). Such an exploration would usually be seen as "adaptive" regression. Adaptive regression operates in the "service of the ego" (Shafii, 1973b). It purportedly leads to a fuller familiarity with one's internal world.

22   Pathological Regression

Adaptive regression can be contrasted with "pathological" regression. The practice of meditation is typically associated with adaptive regression, but it can also lead to pathological regression, i.e. back to primitive psychic functioning with those who are emotionally vulnerable and probably in need of psychotherapy prior to taking up meditation in order to deal with deficits in ego strength. The monotonous repetition of a mantra, the relaxed posture and the reduced sensory input all tend to increase regressive mentation and hence facilitate a relaxation of one's cognitive, e.g. rational and intellectual, defences.

This regression can become pathological with some individuals when it no longer serves healthy ego functions nor *Eros* (love and the life-force) but instead becomes fixated on the id, or worse still, on *Thanatos* (the death-drive, i.e. the wish to return to an undemanding pre-incarnate state). It is thus not surprising that several decades ago Alexander (1931) described meditation as a "sort of artificial schizophrenia with complete withdrawal of libidinal interest from the outside world" (p.30). He is referring to the meditators' attempted non-attachment to desires and drives and to their avoidance of ego-gratification. Here people can be split off emotionally from others, from meaningful relationships and escape from troublesome aspects of social life into isolated self-absorption. This fostered (maladaptive) dissociation between the self and one's surroundings can, for those at risk, lead to de-realisation, as one becomes estranged from once-familiar aspects of the external world. It can also lead to defensive de-personalisation as the (often excessive) meditator may disengage from his or her social domain (and even to some degree from one's personal needs) and thus increasingly withdraw into a minimalist core dissociated from the external trappings of selfhood, and devoid of the necessary motivation to deal with outside demands. The twin effects of such avoiditive de-realisation and de-personalisation can amount to a premature dis-engagement from life in which relationships – both of the "heart" and of work – are neglected in favour of an obsession with the complexity of one's internal space. Here meditation, in some cases, may lead more to self-absorption than to self-awareness. Moreover, the relational aspect of growth may be neglected.

23   Suitability

Not everybody is immediately suitable, i.e. ready for meditation and mindfulness practice (Epstein, 1990). In the West, those who take up meditation tend to be more anxious, neurotic and to report more problems than the population at large (DelMonte, 1990). Those with dissociative identity disorders, as well as psychotic, narcissistic, very shy, schizoid, paranoid and socially phobic individuals, may not readily benefit from meditation. Such people habitually have a range of difficulties in the social domain, i.e. within Lacan's (1966) "Symbolic Order". People whose ability to "read" other people's emotions and to empathise is impaired, may inadvertently come to use meditation as a schizoid defence to escape even further from others and end up feeling even less connected and thus more isolated.

It is therefore argued that the deliberate fostering of non-attachment to the external world, i.e. to mundane reality, may lead to a pathological detachment (or indifference) in those who are already emotionally and socially marginalised. When special techniques such as meditation are used to foster non-attachment and dis-identification this can, for some, have varying de-grees of pathological dissociation and regression as its outcome (Alexander, 1931; Castillo, 1990). This is not to argue against the obvious benefits of adap-tive non-attachment, selective dis-identification and mindfulness as practised by many. However, it does suggest that with more vulnerable individuals, i.e. those with poor ego-strength and emotional deficits, psychotherapy may be indicated initially to help strengthen their ego functioning before they embark upon prolonged meditation practice, as the latter is about learning to side-step identification with one's over-reactionary and ego-centric mind. It should be easier to meditate successfully if one has reasonably well-integrated ego functioning. Paradoxically, one needs considerable ego-strength in order to successfully suspend reactionary ego-functioning by means of meditation.

From a life-span developmental perspective, one needs to first develop one's initially fragile narcissistic "ego" in order to be able to move beyond it to effec-tively embrace the social domain. In other words, it is better to work on one's emotional deficits prior to addressing one's psychodynamic conflicts, there-by rendering it easier to embark upon one's psychosocial growth and spiritual quests. Although there is some overlap, psychotherapy usually progresses from dealing with early developmental deficits, onto exploring psychodynamic con-flicts, before addressing growth issues.

24   Conclusions

In general, practices like meditation, yoga, Gestalt therapy and psychoanalysis, by encouraging quiet mindfulness by means of introspection and circumspec-tion, can, with many people, serve psychological growth (Eros) by encouraging the development of a more reflective self. This can be achieved through explo-rations of: (1) our instinctive and conditioned embodiment, (2) the distorted and furtive aspects of consciousness, (3) the clutching nature of our attach-ments and identifications, and (4) our dogmatic and dualistic thinking. The resultant growth in self-awareness yields perspective and thus should help clarify our deeper values, desires and choices.

However, all techniques can be used inappropriately by the vulnerable. Thus exaggerated self-reflective meditation can encourage dis-engagement and de-motivation with respect to the external world and lead to an escape into an inner-self, to the detriment of social engagement, emotional attach-ments and cathexes. Here the satisfaction associated with either love or work cannot be properly experienced, as the individual, in the premature grasp of Thanatos, forgoes compassion and the interactional aspect of living. Likewise, mindfulness practice may not be suitable for very depressed or psychotic individuals as this practice may only deepen one's disturbed state. There is also the danger of seeking, and achieving, some premature "enlightenment" (partial insight) for those with poor ego strength, as this can be associated with overwhelming levels of psychic re-organisation, abreaction and/or of confusion. The challenge facing all of us as self-conscious and reflective beings is, with the help of the Taoist Yin/Yang metaphor of balance, how to build up and forge an internal sense of self without overly identifying with it; how personally and socially to sustain this fragile sense of self and attain a continuity of deeper identity, while living in the shadow of impermanence and dis-continuity. The ancient practices of meditation, yoga and the like, as well as the contemporary practices of the psychodynamic psychotherapies, offer us some choice out of many possible approaches in dealing with this challenge, but no approach is without its own limits and risks.

Our quest for knowledge and fulfilment has two principal orientations – namely those typified by introversion (Yin) and those by extraversion (Yang). Both are valuable and neither should be neglected. It is a question of equilibrium. Introversion naturally implies introspection and elaboration of our subjectivity or inner world, leading to increased self-awareness, whereas extraversion involves circumspection of the outer world and adaptation to cultural reality, thereby enhancing social awareness and concern. For Jung (1971a) extraverted adaptation to the expectations of social reality more typically occurs during the first half of life. On the other hand, with introspection one is connected inwardly with our essence, i.e. with the mystery of the self (- a microcosm of the universe?). Such introspection tends to become more important to us as we age, but can be precipitated earlier at any stage of life, especially if in crisis.

Circumspection is the *sine qua non* of enhancing our sense of relatedness to external form, i.e. to social convention and to languaging. Inwardness (i.e. subjectivity) and outwardness (i.e. objectivity) can be complementary (Nino, 1997). Put psychodynamically, self-psychology can be balanced by object relations. It may be tempting to escape from harsh external reality by taking refuge inwardly into illusions and even delusions. Likewise, one can remain in exile from one's core-self (essence) by being overly adapted to, and concerned with, external reality, or by developing a false-self or façade. Bridging the chasm between our inner (Yin) and outer (Yang) worlds allows for a two-way flow that enriches both in the process, bringing them more into harmonious alignment. Taoism shows us that all polarities, Yin/Yang dualities, such as between inner and outer, personal and social, earthly and transcendental, and the like, are ultimately illusions, as Yin and Yang are interacting and inter-flowing parts of a non-dualistic whole. A final point is that the Western obsessive focus on individualism, with the forging of a strong individual identity, can create a neurosis around the loss of this over-valued persona or mask. When we identify with this mask, we are identified with a limited, superficial, dualistic and, thus, false self. The more traditional Eastern emphasis on developing a social sense of collective identity, i.e. an awareness of social inter-penetration and of inter-dependence, which does not overly focus on individualism, may facilitate attempts to dis-identify from over-invested egoism.

The aim of meditation, yoga, (and other Eastern techniques) and most forms of depth psychotherapy, especially Jung's Analytical Psychology, is not to become atomised emotional islands, but rather to be more in touch with the personal, social and spiritual aspects of living. Here Jung's (1958) view of the "collective unconscious" is relevant because it embraces much more than just our personal psyche.

Some individuals also use mindfulness meditation to foster a personal opening up to the spiritual domain and as a preparation for a possible after-life or re-incarnation. However, this quest may be enhanced in the here and now by wholeheartedly including the relational aspect of our spirituality in our daily living (as in socially engaged Buddhism), by practising mindful compassion, loving kindness, inter-being and the like. We can thereby evolve our capacity to perceive, and to relate to, the deeper unitary essence – both in ourselves and in others.

The Development of Symbolisation from the Pre-Verbal to the Trans-Verbal: an Evolving Consciousness

1 Introduction

Chapter 4 of this book explores one of the most sophisticated aspects of evolved consciousness, namely the phenomenon of symbolisation. The capacity for symbolisation in humans evolved over hundreds of thousands of years. It also develops in our personal live times, from infancy to mature adulthood.

A symbol is essentially "something which stands for something else". Symbols, including words, images, artefacts, behaviours and rituals, are a complex means of communication that can have multiple levels of meaning. They serve to make tangible and visible the intangible and the invisible – our belief systems, ideas, shared values, hopes and dreams (Womack, 2005).

Symbols can express multi-layered, dense ideas succinctly and economically. The Christian image of Jesus of Nazareth on the cross, for instance, conveys a wealth of historical, religious, spiritual and communal concepts, as does the Virgin Mother and Child.

Ancient Neanderthal cave paintings in Spain, dating back to about 64,000 years ago or more, appear to be the first emergence of the use of symbols by humans. (As Neanderthals could inter-breed with Homo sapiens, we can consider them to be the same species). However, some abstract engravings on a piece of loose ochre in Blombos Cave in South Africa appear to be 77,000 years old, but their meaning remains obscure.

Today, advertising and marketing professionals know the power of symbols to evoke deep and often nameless desires and needs, so they link symbols for Coca-Cola and Nike to suggestions of happiness, achievement, attractiveness and invulnerability.

It has been argued that: "Concepts and words are symbols, just as visions, rituals, and images are; so too are the manners and customs of daily life. Through all of these, a transcendent reality is mirrored. There are so many metaphors reflecting and implying something which, though thus variously expressed, is ineffable; though thus rendered multiform, remains inscrutable. Symbols hold the mind to truth but are not themselves the truth. Hence it is delusory to borrow them. Each civilisation, every age, must bring forth its own." (Zimmer,

1969, pp. 1–2). However in contrast to Zimmer's view, it can also be argued that some symbols are universal, eternal and multi-cultural. Moreover, when Zimmer talks about concepts, visions and images being symbols here, he appears to be referring to internal symbols as opposed to the externalised symbols of the spoken word.

In this final Chapter we address the complex phenomenon of symbolisation both phylogenetically and ontogenetically, i.e., in terms of its archaic and primitive pre-verbal evolutionary origins, as well as developmentally through one's lifespan.

2   Individual Development of Symbolisation

The personal development of symbolisation reflects one's evolving internal psychodynamics, but also involves our social embeddedness or "object relations" and is thus implicated in those "transitional objects" which bridge the gap between our inner and outer worlds.

Our capacity for symbolisation mirrors our experience of apparent reality, as described in Chapter 2, in that it is expressed along a concrete-abstract continuum. Symbolisation can be understood in terms of three developmental, non-discreet, registers along this continuum – the sub-verbal (as in somatisation), the verbal (with the use of linguistic metaphors) and the para-verbal (as in the non-verbal arts such as in drawing, painting, sculpture, architecture, stained-glass, tapestries, music and so on). All of these, in their development, can hint at the existence of a fourth dimension of symbolic expression – namely that of trans-verbal symbolisation. This transcendental dimension is characterised by evoked feelings of timelessness, eternity, infinity – suggesting a universal relevance.

Our ability to create, communicate, understand and share symbols can reflect our level of awareness and psychological integration. This echoes Maslow's hierarchy of needs, where basic safety and survival needs must be met before we can appreciate the higher, more abstract expressions of consciousness such as aesthetics, philosophy and art.

Psychological maturation is a complex process, involving adaptation to the social domain in which we are immersed. For harmonious socialisation we need empathy, for which we need to develop a personal "theory of mind". Fonagy, et al. (1991, 1994) saw the development of a "theory of mind" as emergent from our interactive attachment behaviours with caring others. Being increasingly able to understand one's own inner world facilitates our ability to "read" the wishes, intentions and feelings of others. The increasing

psychosocial competence and fluency within the mental domain – both between and within people – has been called "mentalisation", and is linked very
broadly to mental well-being on a wide range of psychological indicators
(Fonagy, et al., 2011).

Not only do we have to learn to empathise, we also need to learn to communicate sensitively our own intentions, desires and feelings. Symbolic expression can greatly enrich and deepen our reaching out behaviour. With enhanced emotional maturity, there is a parallel developmental sophistication in
our capacity to use symbols within the social domain.

Symbolisation has a broad reach. It expresses numerous archetypal motives
pertaining to the four registers described above, from the sub-verbal (largely
instinctual) right up to the trans-verbal (e.g. the spiritual or mystical) domains.
Para-verbal symbolism is complementary to language and thereby enriches
our search for communion without words. It could thus also be referred to as
the "non-verbal" realm.

3   Symbolisation and Communication

The word "symbol" can be traced back to the Ancient Greek "symbolon" meaning a token or a sign. Its roots are "sym" which stands for "together", and "bal-
lein" meaning "to throw". So "to symbolise" conjures up a metaphorical throwing together of signs to signify something to others.

Symbolisation, being an inter-personal process, is essentially linked to conveying something to other people and thus only happens in a social context.
This can take place in different media and at varying levels of complexity. But
symbols are more than just signs and more than factual communication. For
Carl Jung (1964) signs are always *less* than the concepts that they represent,
whilst the symbol stands for something *more* than its obvious and immediate
meaning: A symbol "hints at something not yet known" (p.41) and has an "as
if" quality about it. Also for Jung "A symbol always presupposes that the chosen expression is the best possible description or formulation of a relatively
unknown fact, which is nonetheless known to exist or is postulated as existing.
..." (Jung, 1971b, p.474).

An actual symbol is frequently a known object which is portrayed in such
a manner so as to be suggestive of something greater than itself, as with a flag
standing for a nation, or a particular dress code for authority or the law, as with
police and judges. This extra dimension often lies at the boundary of awareness, but may also be largely unconscious. Because of this, symbols often allow
one to give some expression to the verbally inexpressible, i.e. to the ineffable.

Symbolisation is not just about any type of communication. It usually involves communicating something meaningful about oneself (as in some forms of creative art), or about the self as part of a larger whole, i.e., about fostering a sense of communion. This collective sense of self contains both a spatial dimension (spreading from the local to the global), and a temporal dimension (ranging from the distant past to eternity). Sacred music and religious art, such as icons, relics and reliquaries spring to mind here as examples of attempted transpersonal symbolisation. This issue shall be addressed later. There can, of course, be an overlap between individual and collective motifs in symbolisation.

Symbolic displays, unlike purely factual and informative communications, tend to be relational and emotionally laden with significance. Transitional objects (such as teddy bears) and self-objects (emotional extensions of the self) are aspects of its development in the context of relating to others (object relations). This aspect shall also be further developed later.

4   Levels of Symbolic Development

The development of symbolisation, like developmental maturation in general, is phasal, involving several overlapping stages. It is postulated here that symbolisation operates in four registers – three of which are quite common, namely the sub-verbal (e.g. hysterical conversions and transitional objects), the verbal (e.g. as in metaphor) and the para-verbal (e.g. as found with dress, icons, art, music, etc.). Keinanen (1998) also referred to three different types of symbols, namely indexical (e.g. simple traffic signs), conventional (or verbal) and the iconic (or pictorial). Like many writers in this area, he focussed mainly on conventional symbolisation.

The most primitive level of symbolisation is in the sub-verbal, e.g. somatic, domain. It is also operates at a relatively low level of awareness. The most esoteric is probably at a trans-verbal or metaphysical level, which we designate as the fourth register. Although we shall begin with the basic sub-verbal level, it must be re-iterated that there is considerable overlap between these four conceptual categories of symbolisation.

We shall first look, very briefly, at symbolisation in an evolutionary context, and thus link its development to an increasing trend in maturational complexity. By now it should be clear that, contrary to a common view, there is no simple equivalence between symbolisation and verbalisation. The latter emerges from "inner speech" (Vygotsky, 1978) and is only one of several avenues of symbolic expression.

5   Pre-Verbal Symbolisation: an Evolutionary Perspective

Aetiology, using the past to explain the present, is the *sine qua non* of the psychologising sciences – from behaviourism to psychoanalysis. The recent growing interest in evolutionary psychology has added phylogeny (evolutionary history) to our descriptions of causality. Phylogeny can thus be perceived of as the "distal" aspect of causality (DelMonte, 2011a). This can be contrasted with ontogeny, one's individual developmental history, which is a description of the "proximate" aspect of causality (Gilbert, 1998a, 1998b).

There has been an evolution of life towards increasing complexity, sophistication and consciousness, culminating in the human capacity for complex conceptualisation. Both phylogenetically (i.e. in evolutionary terms) and ontogenetically (i.e. developmentally) the "thinking-body" almost certainly developed out of the sensory, affective and feeling body. This would imply that both perception and emotion are primary to cognition (in the non-causal but developmental sense). In other words, it is likely that in our evolutionary history (i.e. in our pre-human phylogeny) we were sub-symbolic perceiving and feeling creatures long before we acquired the capacity to think conceptually and to speak. This developmental order also certainly applies to our ontogeny, personal histories, in that language skills, which take time to develop, are secondary to our ability to perceive, vocalise non-verbally (e.g. cry, snort, grunt, whistle, etc.), emote, posture, gesticulate and grimace in social contexts. One could thus say that our personal developmental history (i.e. our ontogeny) recapitulates our collective history (i.e. our phylogeny). Moreover, via sensation and perception we interiorise the external world and construct internal representations and models, e.g. as in cognitive constructs, schemas and imagery.

It has also been observed that the emotional experiences of infants are largely in auditory, imaginal and visual format. These experiences are disproportionately processed and stored in the right hemisphere of the brain during the formative years of brain ontogeny (Semrud-Clikeman and Hynd, 1990). This non-verbal, somatic, emotional and perceptual aspect of construing the world characterises Freud's "primary process" cognition. The verbal and logical construing which is typical of "secondary process" cognition develops later and is mainly a left brain function. Research evidence shows that the right hemisphere matures before the left, a finding which supports Freud's contention that primary process ontogenetically precedes secondary process functions (Schore, 2001). Social attachment behaviours and emotions are also largely a right hemisphere regulation of biological synchronicity between (human) organisms (Schore, 2001).

The evolution of symbolisation from sub-symbolic functioning probably has pre-human origins. In their own primitive way, animals communicate with ritualistic repertoires and "fixed action patterns" (Tinbergen, 1965; Lorenz, 1966; Comfort, 1966; Méry, 1971). Displayed patterns are readily "understood" by the intended observer and the recipient feels prompted or provoked to respond in specific ways. Fish, amphibians, reptiles, birds and mammals all demonstrate specialised behaviours which tend to trigger desired responses in recipients (Tinbergen, 1965; Lorenz, 1966; Méry, 1971; Dixon, 1998; Gilbert, 1998a, 1998b). Mankind also shows archaic vestiges of such interactions, in that particular human displays (e.g. threat, appeasement, seduction, etc.) also tend to precipitate specific emotional and behavioural responses. Both hysterical and projective identification operate as primitive, sub-verbal, interactive mechanisms, which tend to operate at very low levels of cognitive awareness, whereby the emotional unconscious expresses itself symbolically at the non-verbal level.

We shall next discuss both hysterical identification and projective identification in terms of evolutionary theory and also as primitive, i.e. primary process, forms of communication, with implications for both object-relations and symbolisation.

6   Projective Identification

As humans mature, the need to communicate and to symbolise this communication gradually moves from the somatic level on to the socio-verbal. This is a slow developmental process, beginning with inner representation and inner speech, but vestiges of non-verbal communication continue to operate to varying degrees into adulthood. Besides hysterical identification (see below), another example of such a vestige is "projective identification" (Melanie Klein, 1946).

Melanie Klein (1946a) first introduced the term projective identification. She saw it as being the outcome of defensive splitting, in which mostly, but not exclusively, "bad" or unwanted aspects of the self are unconsciously projected into the mother (or later into others such as the therapist) for controlling, manipulating, injuring or possessing her. However, Bion (1962, 1970) understood the wider (i.e. non-defensive) use of projective identification, describing it as an archaic form of communication – akin to the "archaic vestiges" à la Freud. Neither the projector nor the recipient may be consciously aware of this interaction (Buckingham, 2012).

Initially in humans, projective identification emerges in the mother-baby dyad. The pre-verbal infant psychologically projects its needs, fears, anger, desires and wishes by its gesticulations, grimaces, mouth gestures and vocalisations, which are picked up by an attuned mother, or care-giver, as intuitions and so forth. Although this is often a largely an unconscious (or primary) process, it can occur at vague borderline levels of cognitive awareness. When the recipient of these projections reciprocates in the direction prompted by the infant then we can describe this mutuality of feeling and reciprocal role behaviour as projective identification (Bion, 1962, 1970; Ryle, 1994). The infant has projected emotional material, and the mother has identified and complied with it in the desired manner. Although this is often an unconscious (or preconscious) process, one can, over time, develop increasing levels of awareness of this phenomenon.

Such reciprocal role behaviour is also found in many other emotionally laden situations, e.g. between close friends, lovers and among social animals. It also frequently re-emerges in the psychotherapy dyad as transference and counter-transference (see later). In the above examples, both ego-syntonic (agreeable to the self) and ego-dystonic (disagreeable to the self) signals can be projected and unconsciously complied with by the recipient. The recipient of projections can find herself behaving out of character, e.g. by being nudged into having a row, or giving somebody more time in psychotherapy than was intended. With hindsight one can feel manipulated. This is not invariably a disagreeable experience, but one often feels cajoled. However, many Kleinian psychoanalysts continue to see projective identification as a (mainly) pathological evacuation of the patient's unwanted psychic contents.

There is much indirect evidence in support for Bion's view that projective identification may be a form of archaic communication. Phylogenetically, our distant hominid ancestors, like other animals being non-verbal, probably depended on a range of behavioural, facial or acoustic displays in order to communicate. Many basic communicative display patterns have been described, e.g. care eliciting, care seeking, care-giving, consolation, playfulness, mate selection, alliance formation, ranking threats, submission, dependence, sexual attraction, sexual availability, jealousy, aggression, fear, and so forth (Gilbert, 1998a, 1998b; de Waal, 2006, 2013). Such displays trigger strong urges to respond in approach or avoidance ways. This is not surprising, as phylogenetically there would have operated strong selective forces in favour of reciprocal social behaviour, i.e. in favour of primitive non-verbal object-relations. All was not brute competition. Co-operation became increasingly important – especially in terms of group survival and overall may have been more significant than aggressive competition (de Waal, 2006, 2013; Browne, 2013).

Projection and projective identification thus represent very primitive forms of communication and symbolisation. However, there are other non-verbal forms of symbolisation, as found in phobic behaviour (e.g. with respect to snake, coitus and darkness phobias), obsessive-compulsions (e.g., ritual hand washing, compulsive cleaning and checking) and hysteria (e.g. as in hysterical blindness, paralysis and mutism). We shall next look at hysteria in some more detail.

7   Hysterical Identification

As should be obvious by now, non-verbal symbolisation is not confined to the use of external objects, as our own bodies can be "used" symbolically. We do not always need language to communicate our internal experiences, as somatic symbolisation is a powerful means of achieving this. Psychodynamic "hysterical conversions", such as pseudo-epileptic seizures, "glove and stocking" anaesthesia, hysterical dumbness, and "group hysteria", etc., spring to mind here as rather dramatic examples (Freud, 1912, 1930; Szasz, 1972a). This capacity for symbolisation at a very low level of awareness, i.e. at the somatic level is, in evolutionary terms, phylogenetically primitive. It can also be seen in animal behaviour, for example by "playing dead", showing friendliness, displaying dominance and demonstrating submissiveness or neediness. Such behaviour is often socially cohesive or coercive and, thus, adaptive at a group level.

In the absence of language, a capacity for "hysterical", or rather collective, identification allows groups of animals to behave as if they had a "group mind", for example, shoals of fish and dolphins, and flocks of birds or sheep (McDougall, 1921). In this way social animals can share perceptions and affect – e.g. when fleeing from danger, feeding, roosting and mating. Collective behaviour allows access to important higher-order information-processing capabilities that are more difficult, or impossible, to achieve in isolation. Humans, although retaining this capacity, do not need to rely on such "hysterical" identification in order to share feelings, i.e. to show "com-passion", "sym-pathy" or empathy. Yet we sometimes revert to it. With humans, this phenomenon of the 'group mind' has also been referred to as "collective cognition" (Couzin, 2008). It underpins our sociality.

Hysterical identification is conceptually similar to the Kleinian construct of "introjective identification" (Klein, 1946b). The latter probably conveys a more acceptable, i.e. more neutral, image than the popular and traditional connotations associated with "hysteria". However, Klein saw introjective identification as being primarily, but not exclusively, a process of psychologically internalising the benevolent aspects (or "good parts") of others. Such introjective identification can also be seen in less value-laden terms, by stressing its communicative, object-relations and socially adaptive functions. For example, the capacity for a mother to perceive accurately her pre-verbal infant's distress, pain, needs and so forth, is based on the potential for the emotional attunement inherent in introjective identification. Empathy can grow out of such an identificatory process – as does a capacity for "mentalisation" and for developing a "theory of mind" (Liotti and Gilbert, 2011; Fonagy et al., 2011). Without the development of these capacities, object relations are seriously limited. The resulting social isolation leaves the individual vulnerable to adversity.

There is some overlap between introjective and projective identification. They are like two sides of the same coin. What is projected non-verbally by one person can be introjected by another, usually at a low level of awareness. This creates a unity of experience – for better or for worse.

8   Co-Ontogeny, Identification and Transference

Our maturational development is never in social isolation. We thus can describe it as a co-ontogeny or co-development during one's life-span. The mother-child dyad is one such affiliative co-ontogeny. So are long-term social, marital and amicable partnerships, cohorts of siblings, peer groups and so forth.

Phylogenetically, any ease in non-verbal communication would have been selectively advantageous. Pheromones (olfactory hormones) would thus be included here too – especially in social animals and maybe still in humans, although this is controversial. More importantly, those of us who learned to read subtle "body language" cues mediated by bodily posturing, facial grimacing, limb gesticulation, mood displays, etc., would have had a social, and thus a selective and survival, advantage over the socially less discerning. In summary, it paid to be cute, cunning, sensitive and socially alert (Nesse, 1998, Gilbert, 1998a, 1998b; de Waal, 2006, 2013).

Natural selection has thus ensured that we are psycho-neurologically "wired" to display, and be responsive to, somato-social signals or cues. This sometimes operates at a conscious level, e.g. as in empathy, but it can also occur at lower levels of awareness – right down to the unconscious – as is more typical of both projective and introjective identification. In other words, we do not always need to be conscious of our communications. However, such adaptive unconscious communication differs somewhat from the repressed unconscious, in that repression is a psychological defence and is thus typically furtive rather than communicative in nature. We prefer to refer to unconscious communication as part of a psycho-neurological spectrum stretching from the pre-conscious down to the (unrepressed) deep unconscious. The attachment and communication patterns established in early life will pre-figure the type of relationships formed in later life (Lerner, 1989). In other words, the mother-child dyad is the co-ontogenetic prototype of coupling behaviour. Ideally, the "symbiosis" typical of this nurturing dyad forges the crucible or wellspring from which intimacy and affiliation in later adulthood is formed (Bailey and Wood, 1998). This basic relationship is characterised by both introjective and projective identification between mother and child and, as already suggested, is not necessarily as defensive as some Kleinians propose. Rather such projections and introjections serve relational functions with objects, i.e. with people – be they real or imagined.

Mothers and their infants do not need to process all their communications consciously (i.e. at the secondary process level) in order for them to be effective. The same is true of lovers – hence the so-called "irrational" nature of love ("love is blind"). Just as mothers may feel "manipulated" by their infants, psychotherapists can feel similarly manipulated by their patients. Again, this is not necessarily pathological, but it could nevertheless qualify as "primitive", in that it mostly operates at a low level of awareness.

Freud, of course, was very aware of such manipulation in the clinical setting and he referred to this non-verbal correspondence between patient and psychoanalyst as the transference and the counter-transference (Freud, 1900, 1912, 1930). The transference and counter-transference interaction is indicative of unconscious or pre-conscious inter-subjective communication between analyst and analysand. As such it contains aspects of pre-verbal symbolisation, in that particular displays (projections) tend to trigger specific responses at low levels of cognitive awareness. A tendency for this sort of inter-subjective coupling was probably inherited from our phylogenetic past and retained as co-ontogenetic repertoires – such as found in the mother-infant dyad. This natural affiliative tendency has been referred to as "natural transference" by proponents of "kinship therapy" (Bailey and Wood, 1998).

In sum, both projective identification and hysterical (introjective) identification, being forms of non-verbal communication are usually sub-conscious, primitive, but nevertheless "normal" means of somato-social communication and manipulation. They both involve movement towards inter-subjective symmetrisation à la Matte Blanco (Matte Blanco, 1988). Thus, the greater the mutual mental attunement attained within the dyad, the greater the symmetry. This phenomenon has its "pros and cons" in that it can facilitate improved empathy, but it can also lead to a "folie à deux" fusion.

Moreover, such communication can become pathological, for example, when the more conscious aspects of symbolisation fail to develop adequately as one grows up. When there is a failure to thrive psychosocially, communication may largely remain at, or in crises revert to, the primary process and somatic level. The psychic "splits" that characterise the immature, unintegrated personality can result in disowned and unconscious parts of the person being projected into others. For instance, an apparently placid person with denied rage can feel compelled to subtly and covertly instigate conflict in a group, in order to experience their repressed inner discord played out externally. Such defensive denial is typically characterised by psychosomatic and hysterical symptoms.

9   Failures of Symbolisation: Somatisation

As already mentioned, there can be problems in the development of higher order symbolisation. We can thus look at the field of somatoform presentations, i.e., psychosomatic and hysterical disorders where complaints and conflicts are often symbolically manifested in a somatic (physical) format. Patients with somatogenic symptoms tend to be very concrete in their presentation of complaints, due to a rudimentary level of fantasy and a difficulty with verbal symbolisation. In discussing disorders involving psychosomatic symptoms, Kelly (1955) illustrates how the "mind-body" construct can be applied pre-emptively by such patients. This is where people typically show a strong "mind-body" split. The difficulty lies in unnuanced, concrete and dualistic thinking. The person is unable to construe herself as a whole because the body is construed in a "mechanical" manner and the area of mind is construed largely as a separate (i.e. split off) entity. A solution, according to Kelly, for overcoming such mind/body dualism is to be found in (adaptive) regression to early forms of preverbal thinking – "only at that primitive level may we find that the mind and the body were not pre-emptively separated" (Kelly, 1955, p.921). There are several pathways to achieving such adaptive regression – such as found in psychotherapy, psychoanalysis, meditation and hypnosis (DelMonte, 1995, 1997, 1998a, 1998b, 2012).

Pre-verbal construing originates in earliest infancy in order to make sense of those elements of life encountered by the infant in its growth and development. If people later get into serious difficulty while using their more adult construing, their last line of defence is often mal-adaptive regression back to the pre-verbal sense-making of infancy, with its attendant infantile dependency. Hence we often find psychosomatic symptomatology accompanying strong unfulfilled dependency needs. Hysterical symptomatology, likewise associated with dependency needs, often symbolises (painful) unconscious conflicts and deficits, which one defensively avoids because of inherent feelings of shame or guilt.

The psychoanalyst Hogan (1995) presents an interesting comparison between hysterical somatoform conversions, which he sees as post-oedipally symbolic and the more primitive pre-oedipal psychosomatic disorders which, he claims, operate at a lower (i.e. somatic) level of symbolism, with less conscious control. For Hogan, psychosomatic disease of the gut can either represent psychosexual developmental arrest at the oral-anal (i.e. "gut") level, or an emotional regression back to the pre-genital phase following a perceived threat to one's security. In this respect Hogan sees the alexithymia of many psychosomatic patients as a defence against the shame felt about conflictual fantasies and aggressive feelings by blocking their conscious verbalisation. Instead these negative impulses are directed inwards to produce "masochistic gratification in the pain of psychosomatic symptoms" (p.103). This alleged masochism, coupled with alexithymia and/or other defensive or communicative postures, makes psychosomatic disorders difficult but not impossible to treat (Hogan, 1995; DelMonte, 1995, 1998a, 1998b, 2000b). Luckily, most people manage to move beyond the dependency and somatic symbolisation of subverbal infancy to develop verbal and para-verbal symbolic expression such as found in artistic painting or music. But this developmental journey requires some emotional support.

10   Transitional Objects

As is clear from the above discussion thus far, the capacity for primitive symbolic expression commences in pre-verbal childhood. We are all familiar with the observation that infants can demonstrate strong emotional attachment to objects like an old blanket. Such items have been called "transitional objects" by Winnicott (1971). He saw such pieces of old blanket as representing "the infant's transition from a state of being merged with the mother to a state of being in relation to the mother as something outside and separate" (pp.14–15). Transitional objects are thus "symbolical of some part-object, such as the breast" (p.6). We can thus conclude that the use of transitional objects is normal and healthy at the pre-genital stage.

Kohut's (1977) construct of a "self-object" is similar to that of a transitional object. Self-objects are objects (including people) "out there" that are experienced emotionally as being an extended part of the self. In this sense both self-objects and transitional objects are functionally symbolic of an attachment between self and (m)other. However, self-objects can be found at both the pre- and post-oedipal phases. Transitional objects, in particular, are perceived as symbolising a desire to maintain some felt unity between a child and its mother, while taking its first steps towards separation. Here the transitional object, a pre-verbal (often oral) symbol, functions to reduce separation anxiety by "communicating" to the child a sense of remaining in touch with its principal care-giver. Religious art and artefacts, depicting a caring God, benevolent saints or guardian angels who watch over and protect us, fulfil a similar emotional function for many religious people.

Wright (1998) has argued that transitional objects only occupy a transitional place in symbolic development as they are "not yet separate enough to be fully fledged symbols" (p.453). By fully-fledged symbols Wright has verbal symbols in mind, reflecting a discernible stance, found among many psychotherapists and psychoanalysts, valuing verbal over non-verbal symbolisation.

The use of transitional objects in the development of symbolisation does not always occur without problems. According to Winnicott, fetishes can be seen as transitional objects which have been carried forward into the post-genital phase. (Also see Storr, 1965, 1972). Likewise male transvestism can betray a lingering need to remain identified with and erotically attached to mother by means of transitional objects in the form of female clothing.

11 Symbolic "Castration"

Francoise Dolto linked symbol formation to successful psychodynamic "castration" in the psychoanalytic sense (Dolto, 1982). An important step in this journey is the psychological rupture of the "umbilical connection" which Dolto referred to as "umbilical castration". Its failure leads to unresolved fusional states of dependency between mother and child, which, according to Dolto, can later manifest as "psychoses" and "phobias", including agoraphobia and panic disorder.

The first step in separation seen to be conducive to symbol formation by Dolto is "oral castration" – as linked to weaning and its sequelae – the first move away from maternal dependency. Then comes "anal castration" via toilet training with its focus on cleanliness, control and order. Finally, there is the classical or phallic castration via resolution of the Oedipus complex, when, for example, a little boy acknowledges that the main romantic bond is between his two parents by surrendering his primary claim to mother.

Dolto sees the pleasure linked to oral, anal and phallic drives as capable of being "inserted into a longer circuit" (by postponed gratification), thereby acquiring some symbolic expression. The primitive tendency towards a

short circuit satisfaction of drives is, initially, elongated into a longer circuit by way of transitional objects as described above. Successful "symbolic
castration", according to Dolto, leads to instinctual drives being given satisfaction and expression at a higher level of symbolism. A few obvious examples readily come to mind here. To begin with, oral drives can be satisfied
in speech, singing, literature, poetry, and the like. Anal drives can be transformed into manual skills, as in handcrafts, pottery and sculpture as well as
into hygienic and organisational needs. Phallic drives can be expressed in
exhibitionistic professions such as ballet, acrobatics, acting and, maybe, in
football and car-racing.

Dolto stresses that such symbolic castration should not be conducted in a
brutal or frustrating way by harsh parenting, i.e., by a "castrating" father. Infantile strivings for pleasure and satisfaction should gradually and caringly be
transmuted, rather than suppressed aggressively.

12   Sublimation

Dolto's position is essentially Freudian. The extension of short-circuit satisfaction into a longer circuit via the insertion of transitional objects should eventually lead on to the sublimation, in the Freudian sense, of basic drives into
higher order symbolic activity. For Freud, the creative arts owe their existence
to the sublimation of instinctual impulses (Freud, 1930). However, not everybody is content to see symbolisation and creativity in this light. Anthony Storr
(1972, 1992) has argued against the view that Freudian sublimation is the sole
source of our creativity.

However, Storr does concede that schizoid and obsessional personality
structures, with their characteristic defences allow, in part at least, for particular manifestations of creativity via sublimation. Of particular interest to
symbolisation are obsessional rituals. Storr argues that when "a child begins
to perform his own rituals, he is asserting his ability to protect himself against
the dangers of both outer and inner worlds, rather than demanding that his
parents shall do it for him. The rituals are serving the function of easing the
transition from the complete dependency of earliest childhood to the partial
independence of the latency period" (Storr, 1972, p.128).

So here we see rituals as performing a role similar to that of transitional
objects. However, as childhood proceeds into adulthood such obsessional rituals become increasingly symbolised. Thus the ritual is more than a
means of defence – "but also a means of transmuting instinctive impulses to give them expression in less direct and more acceptable ways" (Storr,

1972, p.144). This is akin to Dolto's observation that such impulses can be put on a long-circuit, or "sustained" rather than acted out as Heimann (1950) described it. Given the obsessionals' distaste for, and distancing attitude towards, basic impulses such as aggression and sexuality it is not surprising that many creatively gifted people like Stravinsky were highly obsessional (Storr, 1972).

13 Dreaming and Verbal Symbolisation

No discussion on symbolisation can side-step the phenomenon of dreaming. Dreaming is replete with symbolic function. Freud (1900) and later Jung (1964) wrote extensively on the symbolism inherent in dreaming. It is not our intention to review their extensive writings here, as this has been done so often before. In brief, it can be argued that dreaming facilitates the conversion of bodily, emotional and somatic construing (e.g. instinctual impulses, wishes and desires) into a post-somatic level of expression. Freud would have seen dreaming as a "primary process" and thus closely linked to other unconscious processes – including somatisation. Deliberate reflection on the primary process symbolic contents of our dreams, often facilitated by "dream interpretation" during psychoanalysis, facilitates their symbolisation at a verbal level. Such rational, conscious verbalisation is characteristic of the Freudian "secondary process". Of course, secondary process thinking usually develops naturally and its genesis does not require professional dream interpretation! Symbolisation, as found in dreams, facilitates internal psychic responsivity and accommodation to the demands of the outside world, i.e. of object relations. In other words, the internal pleasure principle or wish fulfilment aspect of dream symbolisation partially submits to the external "reality principle" while dreaming (Freud, 1900, 1912, 1930).

The transition from primary to secondary process representation is an important step in symbolic development. As mentioned earlier, somatic symbolisation, being sub-verbal, is seen as primary process sense-making and communication. Initially, as infants, we construe all reality at the pre-verbal, perceptual and somatic level. Then one increasingly goes on to construct a sense of social reality at the level of linguistic symbolism – namely by developing cognitive constructs (or secondary process cognition in Freudian terms). Hence, the "talking body" developmentally emerges out of an embodied sensory-affective infancy, bathed in a social context, i.e. in the Symbolic Order (Lacan, 1966). We have already referred to a similar process occurring phylogenetically, in the slow evolution of the human species itself, as language emerges out of sensory-affective pre-linguistic hominids. Ontogeny recapitulates phylogeny!

14   Lacan and the Symbolic Order

In evolutionary terms, both projective and introjective identification, as well as "languaging", are adaptive insofar as they facilitate inter-subjective communion. The difference between these identifications and "languaging" is that speech can operate at a much "higher" and more abstract level of symbolism, representing an adaptation to the "Symbolic Order" (society) à la Lacan. Lacan (1966) in his writings dealt with three orders – the "Real", the "Imaginary" and the "Symbolic". Put very simply, the "Real" is the given, but essentially unknowable, unsymbolisable reality in all its complexity stretching to beyond human perception; the "Imaginary" is a mentally constructed, personal, inner representation of the world (and of our bodies); and entering into the "Symbolic" order is operating within the stipulations of socio-political reality, which is enriched by the use of verbal (and other) symbols in our direct and not so direct communications.

15   Society and Verbal Symbolisation

As already stated, one gradually learns to use language in a social context. In order to talk with others about experiences (e.g. feelings of anger, envy or nausea) we need to use verbal labels ("putting verbal form on feelings"). The usage of such labels means that much primary sense-making gradually acquires a secondary, i.e. cognitive or more abstract overlay, as we build up our inner representational worlds in response to external demands. Their contents can be expressed via complex languaging behaviour with its attendant verbal symbolisation. Among its richest expressions are found the exquisite works of literary genius, such as those of Dante, Shakespeare, and Proust. The symbolism of poetry adds an extra, looser, dimension to language that is often more difficult to express in straight prose.

Mathematical symbols, usually but not always, verbalisable, can be seen as a special numerical category of verbal symbols. These range from common everyday numerals, to complex algebraic equations, geometric formulae, and on to the complex formulae of theoretical physics, with their more specialised social application. However, mathematical symbols, once understood, do not depend on a particular language such as English in order to be communicated.

In a sense mathematics is a universal form of symbolisation, now used across the globe - as are the symbols of music.

16   Para-Verbal Symbolisation

So far we have focussed, in the main, on symbolisation at both the pre-verbal (somatic) and verbal levels. However, iconic symbolisation can side-step the verbal. It is, in part, concerned with imagery and is found in the visual arts such as drawing, painting, sculpture and, of course, architecture. But artistic symbolisation is not confined to the visual arts. It also finds expression in the wide varieties of music which have existed throughout the ages.

Symbolisation has always been inherent to the arts. This is still the case to-day as there is so much of value here that is not readily within the expressive reach of the empirical sciences. The logical positivism (Compte, 1855) of the scientific method of inquiry cannot be applied easily to so much of what is culturally pertinent to us – as not everything is easily subjected to measurement (DelMonte, 2000c). "A symbol, by its very nature, refers to an absent reality" (Gibson, 1995, p.21). Artistic symbolisation attempts to reach "beyond the narrow field of the given" (Gibson, p.22), to give expression to an unknown quality in human experience. We need symbols to help communicate those aspects of life that fall outside of the competence of the language and methods of science.

Artistic symbolisation over the ages has covered a very broad range of expression and has also served many functions. It can also function therapeutically by reaching us where words may not be adequate (de Botton and Armstrong, 2013). Artistic symbolisation is more holistic and analogous than the digital symbolism of much of the sciences. At a basic level, artistic symbolisation can be seen as no more than a substitute (compensation) for those who have difficulty verbalising their internal representations and emotions, as may be found with some musicians and painters. However, much symbolisation can also be an expression of the verbally ineffable and of sheer genius, as witnessed in the works of individuals such as the composer Ludwig van Beethoven and the artist Rembrandt van Rijn.

17   Trans-Verbal Symbolisation

Is there symbolisation pointing beyond the "hic et nunc" (here and now) of the embodied domain and beyond the ephemerality of uttered speech, or pointing beyond the fashion-dependent latest craze in art or music? In other words, does symbolisation ever hint at a transcendent reality, to enter the felt time-lessness and unboundedness of spirituality? In our view, universal symbols which appear to survive the test of time, i.e. which "speak" to us regardless of place or time, no matter where or when they were produced, can be labelled trans-verbal. They are also archetypal in the Jungian sense (Jung, 1958b, 1964). Here one is less concerned with communication but more with communion. Whereas words facilitate the former, a sense of communion can be fostered non-verbally (DelMonte, 1995). Historically, most artistic symbols were reli-gious and more concerned with "why" rather than "how" questions. They had the purpose of uniting the world of the senses with that of the meta-physical and the spiritual, as, for example, in early Celtic spirituality (Streit, 1984). Celtic crosses come to mind here, with the horizontal line symbolising the Earth, the vertical line the Heavens and the circle Divine Unity.

Some lines of poetry, works of art and pieces of music shall continue to strike a chord with many of us as they constitute "texts" which are less context-bound. Their relevance to us does not depend on the current trends in art, music or poetry. They also tend towards the ineffable and the immanent. In a way, such symbols are seemingly unchanging and are less time-dependent. In a metaphorical sense, they are neither of the body nor of the mind – yet they resonate therein. In sum, they can be seen as metaphysical.

The spiritual domain, purportedly, lies beyond the physical, mental and so-cial domains, while yet infusing all three. The Chinese call it "Yuan Shen" – the source of life lying beyond conceptualisation. Being ineffable, Yuan Shen is beyond words – and thus cannot be verbally symbolised (DelMonte, 2000c). Bion referred to this ultimate unknowable reality as "O", and as the "absolute truth", the "infinite" and the "thing-in-itself" (Bion, 1970, p. 26). For Lacan (1966) this is the "Real". Matte Blanco (1988) would call this the domain of "Absolute Symmetry" where no contrasts or distinctions can be cognitively discerned. All of this suggests that the spiritual can only be loosely symbolised, para-verbally, e.g. with music, dance, painting and the like. Such symbols are no more than "fingers pointing at the moon" – indicating a vague direction and hinting at a reality beyond direct human perception. The mystical quality of the spiritual domain leaves its apologists open to the charge of solipsism. But given the brevity and finitude of our individual lives, humankind shall remain curious about the transpersonal, i.e., about the eternal and the infinite, beyond our little selves.

In both Oriental and Christian meditation, mantras are seen to have transpersonal symbolic value. They can be envisaged as being utilised as tran-sitional "objects" between the self and the non-self (or spiritual domain). In other words, mantras as transitional objects serve a transcendental function, helping to release the mind from ego grasping, so as to achieve the "no-mind" tranquillity, beyond all symbolisation (DelMonte, 1995, 1998a, 1998b).

18   Summary and Conclusions

Symbolisation is a bridge between subjective internal psychic reality and the demands of external object-relations. Its development begins in pre-verbal infancy. Both introjective and projective identification are aspects of pre-verbal, primary process (i.e. rudimentary) symbolic communication. Symbolisation may, in certain circumstances, become stuck at the pre-verbal level, as with somatoform disorders. However, most individuals develop a reasonably sophisticated capacity for verbal symbolisation with a progressive unfolding of their linguistic skills. This process can be assisted by the psychodynamic psychotherapies. Verbalisation is an expression of conscious, secondary process symbolisation, but it rarely escapes the assistance of non-verbal cues as found in posturing, grimacing, gesticulating and miming.

Many individuals, however, rely less on verbalisation and feel a greater affinity for the symbolic value of painting, sculpture and music. Such para-verbal symbolic expression is further developed in the domain of trans-verbal symbolisation – perhaps its ultimate expression? Symbolic expression encompasses a huge range, in that it strives to express that which lies beyond or below self-evident reality. Herein we include the repressed unconscious, the psycho-neurological (adaptive) unconscious, the pre-conscious and the trans-conscious. The latter transcendent quality of symbolism is the essence of the age-old ineffable mystical experiences which have both perplexed the enriched the human condition. But there are limits to what can be symbolised. Symbols can only point in the direction of the Real – but can never be equated with it. Yet trans–verbal symbolisation appears to be the ultimate expression of consciousness. A sense of the trans-verbal can often be accessed during spiritual practices, including meditation and mindfulness, as well as in wondrous landscapes, skyscapes, seascapes and the like, and through the great arts such as in music, painting and sacred architecture, to name but a few.

Conclusion

This book has taken us on a very long multi-disciplinary journey indeed – from the initial Big Bang to the symbolic, metaphysical and interpersonal domains of humans! Curiosity about all aspects of our place in Nature and in the Cosmos has driven the inquiry which led to this book. We see mind and its evolution as being central to the human condition, to the quest for meaning and to the fulfilment of a meaningful life.

We have traced evolution from its very beginnings in the evolution of matter to the evolution of life itself and of the mind. Some, if not most of what is written has to be provisional, as most ideas become refined and even outdated or redundant over time. This has been particularly true of scientific theories in the past, and is very likely to continue into the future. Philosophical and spiritual views are more robust but also tend to change over time. Nevertheless, they tend remain relevant to us to a much greater degree than scientific discoveries, as the latter often become dislodged by new findings and theories. Mysteries remain, especially about the nature of black holes, dark matter and dark energy. Our physical universe appears to be expanding more and more rapidly, but so is current cultural evolution. Many of today's ideas and theories may eventually be surpassed!

However, just think of the ancient Greek and Eastern philosophies and how people still consult them. Who pays much attention to outdated scientific "facts", such as alchemy or the belief that the Earth was the centre of the universe? Metaphysical speculations will always be part of the human mind, but they, by their very nature, are very difficult to put to the scientific test. Nevertheless, it would be wrong to dismiss the importance of the sciences and of its main focus, namely matter. Vast progress has been made in our understanding of the Cosmos, genetics, epi-genetics, evolution, physics, neuroscience and so forth.

Based on what science, philosophy, psychology, the wisdom traditions and theories of mind have thought us, we endeavour to apply our current understandings of the human condition to the alleviation of unnecessary suffering. Psychotherapy plays an important role here, as does the beauty of nature and the arts. For many people religious experience and expression remain of central importance. Consciousness is the critical medium of the human condition. We argue that consciousness, together with matter, are primary in that they, most likely, have evolved together. Here we agree with the pre-Socratic Greek philosopher, Heraclitus, that there is a fundamental unity in what appears to

© KONINKLIJKE BRILL NV, LEIDEN, 2019 | DOI:10.1163/9789004408753_007 be opposite. We postulate that this view also applies to our deeper understanding of mind and matter.

Our ethical awareness has also progressed in so many diverse domains such as our approach to gender, animals, disability, ethnic and religious minorities, as is evident from the study of paleo-anthropology and paleo-compassion. Both scientists and philosophers strive to know the Truth. Psychoanalysts endeavour to make the unconscious conscious. As we, mere humans, are unlikely to ever know the Real in its full complexity we are compelled to dwell in mysteries and delightful doubts!

Bibliography

Abed, R. T. (1998). The Sexual Competition Hypothesis for Eating Disorders. *British Journal of Medical Psychology*, 71(4), 525–547.

Al-Khalili, J. and McFadden, J. (2014). *Life on the Edge: The Coming of Age of Quantum Biology.* London: Transworld Publishers.

Al-Khalili, J. (2016). *Lost Horizons: The Big Bang.* BBC4 TV, 17th January.

Al-Khalili, J. (2017). *Quantum Mechanics.* London: Ladybird Books.

Alexander, F. (1931). Buddhist training as an artificial catatonia (the biological meaning of psychic occurrences). *Psychoanalytic Review*, 18, 129–145.

Ameisen, J. C. (2012). *Sur les Épaules de Darwin.* Paris: Editions Les Liens Qui Liberent.

Ardal, G. and Hammar, A. (2011). Is impairment in cognitive inhibition in the acute phase of major depression irreversible? Results from a 10-year follow up. *Psychology and Psychotherapy: Theory, Research and Practice*, 84(2), 141–150.

Arhem, P. and Liljenstrom, H. (1997). On the co-evolution of cognition and consciousness. *Journal of Theoretical Biology*, 187, 601–612.

Assagioli, R. (1965). *Psychosynthesis: A Manual of Principles and Techniques.* New York: Hobbs, Duram and Co.

Aurobindo, S. (1973). *The Supramental Manifestation upon Earth.* Pondicherry, India: Ashram Press.

Bailey, K. G. and Wood, H. E. (1998). Evolutionary Kinship Therapy: Basic principles and treatment implications. *British Journal of Medical Psychology*, 71(4), 509–523.

Balint, M. (1958). The three areas of the mind. *International Journal of Psycho-Analysis*, 39, 328–340.

Barnes-Holmes, D; Cochrane, A; Barnes-Holmes, Y; Stewart, A. (2004). "Offer it up" and psychological acceptance: Empirical evidence for your grandmother's wisdom? *Irish Psychologist*, 31(3), 72–78.

Barrow, J. and Tipler, F. (1988). *The Anthropic Cosmological Principle.* Oxford: Oxford University Press.

Bateson, G. (1972). *Steps to an Ecology of Mind.* New York: Ballantine Books.

Behe, M. (2004). Irreducible complexity: An obstacle to Darwinian evolution. In W. A. Dembski and R. Ruse (Eds.). *Debating Design: From Darwin to D.N.A.* Cambridge, U.K: Cambridge University Press.

Bion, W. R. (1962). *Learning from Experience.* London: Heineman.

Bion, W. R. (1970). *Attention and Interpretation.* London: Tavistock.

Bion, W. R. (1974). *Brazilian Lectures.* São Paulo: Imago.

Birtchnell, J. (1995). Exercising caution in applying animal models to humans: A response to Price and Gardner. *British Journal of Medical Psychology*, 68(3), 207–210.

Birtchnell, J. (1997). Attachment in an interpersonal context. *British Journal of Medical Psychology*. 70(3), 265–279.

Bogdanov, I. and Bogdanov, G. (2010), G. *Le Visage de Dieu*. Paris: Grasset.

Bravesmith, A. (2012). Silence lends integrity to speech: Transcending the opposites of speech and silence in the analytic dialogue. *British Journal of Psychotherapy*, 28(1), 21–34.

Brewin, C. R. and Andrews, B. (1997). Reasoning about repression: Inferences from clinical and experimental data. In M. Conway (Ed.), *Recovered Memories and False Memories*. Oxford: Oxford University Press, pp. 192–205.

Broad, C. (1925). *The Mind and its Place in Nature*. London: Routledge and Kegan Paul.

Bronfenbrenner, U. (2005). *Making Human Beings Human: Bioecological Perspectives on Human Development*. California: SAGE Publications, Inc.

Brown, D. P. and Engler, J. (1980). The stages of mindfulness meditation: A validation study. *Journal of Transpersonal Psychology*, 12 (2), 143–192.

Brown, J. F. (2002). Epistemological differences within psychological science: A philosophical perspective on the validity of psychiatric diagnoses. Psychology and Psychotherapy: Theory, Research and Practice, 75, 239–250.

Browne, I. (2013). *The Writings of Ivor Browne: Steps along the Road: The Evolution of a Slow Learner*. Cork: Cork University Press.

Bruckner, P. (2000). *L'Euphorie Perpetuelle*. Paris: Grasset.

Buckingham, L. (2012). A thread in the labyrinth: Returning to Melanie Klein's concept of projective identification. *British Journal of Psychotherapy*, 28(1), 3–20.

Burnham, T. and Phelan, J. (2001). *Mean Genes*. London: Penguin Books.

Capra, F. and Luisi, P. L. (2014). The Systems View of Life: A Unifying Vision. Cambridge: Cambridge University Press.

Carter, C. O. (1970). *Human Heredity*. London: Penguin Books.

Carey, T. J. (2005). Evolution, depression and counselling. *Counselling Psychology Quarterly*, 18(3), 215–222.

Carrington, P. and Ephron, H. S. (1975). Meditation as an adjunct to psychotherapy. In S. Ariety and G. Chrzanowski (Eds.), *New Dimensions in Psychiatry: A World View*. New York: John Wiley and Sons.

Castillo, R. J. (1990). Depersonalisation and meditation. *Psychiatry*, 53, 158–168.

Cavalli-Sforza, L. L. (2000). *Genes, Peoples and Languages*. London: The Penguin Press.

Chalmers, D. J. (2010). *The Character of Consciousness*. Oxford: Oxford University Press.

Chalmers, D. J. (2012). *Constructing the World*. Oxford: Oxford University Press.

Clark, J. E. (1997). A dynamical systems perspective on the development of a complex ` adaptive skill. In C. Dent-Read and P. Zukow-Goldring (Eds.) *Evolving Explanations of Development: Ecological Approaches to Organism – Environment Systems*, pp.383–406; Washington: American Psychological Association. Collins and Sons.

Coltart, M. (1992). *Slouching Towards Bethlehem: And Further Psychoanalytic Explorations.* London: Free Association Books.

Comfort, A. (1966). *Nature and Human.* London: Penguin.

Comte, A. (1855). The positive philosophy, In *Language, Man and Society.* New York: Ams Press, 1974.

Couzin, I. (2008). Collective cognition in animal groups. *Trends in Cognitive Science,* 13(1), 36–43.

Crepmair, L., Mitterlehner, F., Loew, T., Bachler, E., Rother, W. and Nickel, M. (2007). Promoting mindfulness in psychotherapists in training influences the treatment results of their patients: A randomized double-blind controlled study. *Psychotherapy and Psychosomatics,* 76, 332–338.

Creswell, D. (2008). Mindfulness meditation slows progression of HIV. *Brain Behavior, and Immunity,* 22(6), 797–1008.

Dalai Lama, (2002). *The Dalai Lama's Little Book of Inner Peace.* London: Harper Collins.

Dolto, F. (1982). *Séminaire de Psychanalyse D'Enfants.* Paris: Seuil.

Damasio, A. (2018). *The Strange Order of Things: Life, Feeling and the Making of Cultures.* New York: Penguin Random House.

Damasio, A. and Carvalho, G. B. (2013). The nature of feelings: Evolution and neurological origins. *Nature Reviews. Neuroscience,* 14(2), 143–152.

Darlington, C. D. (1966). *Genetics and Man.* London: Allen and Unwin.

Davey, J. (1981). Once upon a time. *Observer Review,* 16th August, pp.19–21.

Davidson, R. J; Kabat-Zinn, J; Schumacher, J; Rosenkranz, M. S; Muller, D; Santorelli, S. F; Urbanowski, F; Harrington, A; Bonus, K. and Sheridan, J. F. (2003). Alterations in brain and immune function produced by mindfulness meditation. *Psychosomatic Medicine,* 65, 564–570.

Dawkins, R. (1976). *The Selfish Gene.* Oxford: Oxford University Press.

Dawkins, R. (2006). *The God Delusion.* London: Bantam Press.

De Botton, A. (2003). *The Art of Travel.* London: Penguin Books.

De Botton, A. and Armstrong, J. (2013). *Art as Therapy.* London: Phaidon Press.

De Mello, A. (1990). *Awareness.* Michigan: Zondervan.

De Silva, P. (1990). Buddhist psychology: A review of theory and practice. *Current Psychology,* 9(3), 236–254.

De Waal, F. (2006). *Primates and Philosophers: How Morality Evolved.* New Jersey: Princeton University Press.

De Waal, F. (2013). *The Bonobo and the Atheist: In Search of Humanism among the Primates.* New York: Norton.

Deatherage, G. (1975). The clinical use of mindfulness meditation techniques in short-term psychotherapy. *Journal of Transpersonal Psychology,* 7 (2), 133–134.

DelMonte, M. M. (1981). Suggestibility and meditation. *Psychological Reports,* 48, 727–737.

DelMonte, M. M. (1984a). Response to meditation in terms of physiological, behavioural and self-report measures. *International Journal of Psychosomatics*, 31 (2), 3–17.

DelMonte, M. M. (1984b). Meditation: Similarities with hypnoidal states and hypnosis. *International Journal of Psychosomatics*, 31(3), 24–34.

DelMonte, M. M. (1985). Anxiety, defensiveness and physiological responsivity in novice and experienced meditators. *International Journal of Eclectic Psychotherapy*, 4(1+2), 1–13.

DelMonte, M. M. (1987). A constructivist view of meditation. *American Journal of Psychotherapy*, 41(2), 286–298.

DelMonte, M. M. (1989a). A brief outline of the views of existentialist- phenomenological writers and how their views relate to psychotherapy. *Psychologia*, 32, 81–90.

DelMonte, M. M. (1989b). Existentialism and psychotherapy: A constructivist perspective. *Psychologia*, 32(2), 81–90.

DelMonte, M. M. (1990). The relevance of meditation to clinical practice: An overview. *Applied Psychology: An International Review*, 39(3), 331–354.

DelMonte, M. M. (1991). The use of non-verbal construing and metaphor in psychotherapy. *International Journal of Psychosomatics*, 38(1–4), 68–75.

DelMonte, M. M. (1995a). Meditation and the unconscious. *Journal of Contemporary Psychotherapy*, 25(3), 223–242.

DelMonte, M. M. (1995b). Silence and emptiness in the service of healing: Lessons from meditation. *British Journal of Psychotherapy*, 11(3), 368–378.

DelMonte, M. M. (1996). Systems theory and psychotherapy: A constructivist perspective. In M. G. T. Kwee and T. L. Holdstock (Eds.), *Western and Buddhist Psychology: Clinical Perspectives*. Delft: Eburon Publishers, pp. 269–293.

DelMonte, M. M. (1997). Psychotherapy: Science or Mysticism? Paper presented at symposium organised by the Austrian Forum for Theoretical Psychology entitled, "Ways of thinking, understanding and knowing: Bridging the gap between science, humanities and mysticism", Vienna.

DelMonte, M. M. (1998a). The embodied mind, the talking cure and the silence of meditation. In M. DelMonte and Y. Haruki (Eds.), *The Embodiment of Mind: Eastern and Western Perspectives*. Delft: Eburon Publishers, pp.129–139.

DelMonte, M. M. (1998b). The mind versus matter debate. In M. DelMonte and Y. Haruki (Eds.), *The Embodiment of Mind: Eastern and Western Perspectives*. Delft: Eburon Publishers, pp. 17–20.

DelMonte, M. M. (2000a). Retrieved memories of childhood sexual abuse. *British Journal of Medical Psychology*, 73, 1–13.

DelMonte, M. M. (2000b). Non-attachment, dis-identification and dissociation in meditation, Qi-gong and hypnosis: mal-adaptive Adaptive or mal-adaptive? In Wang Weidong, Yugi Sasaki and Yutaka Haruki (Eds.), *Bodywork and Psychotherapy in the East*. Delft: The Netherlands, Eburon.

DelMonte, M. M. (2000c). Psychotherapy: Science or Mysticism? In F. Wailmer, G. Fleck and K. Edlinger (Eds.), *Science, Humanities and Mysticism: Complementary Perspective*. Vienna, Braumuller Publications, pp. 111–121.

DelMonte, M. M. (2001a). Evolutionary psychology: Does mind matter or is it immaterial? *Journal of Critical Psychology, Counselling and Psychotherapy*, 1(4), 217–229.

DelMonte, M. M. (2001b). Fact or fantasy? A review of recovered memories of childhood sexual abuse. *Irish Journal of Psychological Medicine*, 18(3), pp. 99–105.

DelMonte, M. M. (2001c). Symbolisation: Its development from the pre-verbal to the trans-verbal. *Journal of Critical Psychology, Counselling and Psychotherapy*, 1(1), 32–44.

DelMonte, M. M. (2003). Mindfulness and the de-construction of attachments. *Constructivism in the Human Sciences*, 8(2), 151–171.

DelMonte, M. M. (2004). Ways of understanding: Meditation, mysticism and science – bridging the gap between East and West. In M. Blows, S. Srinivasan, J. Blows, P. Bankart, M. DelMonte and Y. Haruki (Eds.), *The Relevance of the Wisdom Traditions in Contemporary Society. The Challenge of Psychology*. Delft: The Netherlands, Eburon Publishers, pp. 1–23.

DelMonte, M. M. (2005). Evolutionary psychopathology: What is the matter with mind? *Constructivism in the Human Sciences*, 10, 145–164.

DelMonte, M. M. (2009). Empty thy mind and come to thy senses: A de-constructive path to inner peace. In E. Franco (Ed.), *Yogic Perception, Meditation and Altered States of Consciousness*. Vienna: Austrian Academy of Sciences, pp. 449–479.

DelMonte, M. M. (2011a). Post-Darwinian psychology: Does mind really matter? *The International Journal of Healing and Caring*, 11 (1), 1–23.

DelMonte, M. M. (2011b). Mindfulness: Psychodynamic Perspectives. *Paradoxia: Journal of Nondual Psychology*, 3, 1–26.

DelMonte, M. M. (2012). Mindfulness and awareness: Constructivist, psychodynamic and Eastern perspectives. *International Journal of Mental Health and Addiction*, 10(3), 311–329.

DelMonte, M. M. and Halpin, M. (2014). Understanding Meditation. In M. Halpin (Ed.) *How to be Happy and Healthy - the Seven Natural Elements of Mental Health*. Dublin: Ashfield Press.

DelMonte, M. M. and Kenny, V. (1985a). Models of Meditation. *British Journal of Psychotherapy*, 1(3), 197–214.

DelMonte, M. M. and Kenny, V. (1985b). An overview of the therapeutic effects of meditation. *Psychologia*, 28(4), 189–202.

Dixon, A. K. (1998). Ethological strategies for defense in animals and humans: Their role in some psychiatric disorders. *British Journal of Medical Psychology*, 71(4), 417–445.

Dworkin, B. R., Filewich, R. J., Miller, N. E., Craigmyle, N. and Pickering, T. G. (1979). Baroreceptor activation reduces reactivity to noxious stimulation: Implications for hypertension. *Science*, 205, 1299–1301.

Epstein, M. (1990). Psychodynamics of meditation: Pitfalls on the spiritual path. *Journal of Transpersonal Psychology*, 22(1), 17–34.

Epstein, S. (1983). The unconscious, the pre-conscious, and self-concept. In J. Suls and A. G. Greenwald (Eds.). Psychological Perspectives of the *Self, Vol. 2*. London: L.E.A. Publishers, pp 291–247.291–349.

Faer, L. M; Hendricks, A; Abed, R. T. and Figueredo, A. J. (2005). The evolutionary psychology of eating disorders: Female competition for mates or for status? *Psychology and Psychotherapy: Theory, Research and Practice*, 78, 397–417.

Ferry, L. (2006). *Apprendre à Vivre*. Paris: Plon.

Fisher, S. and Greenberg, R. P. (1996). *Freud Scientifically Reappraised*. New York: John Wiley and Sons.

Fleury, V. (2006). *De L'Oeuf à l'éternité: Le Sens de L'évolution*. Paris: Flammarion.

Fonagy, P., Bateman, A. and Bateman, A. (2011). The widening scope of mentalizing: A discussion. *Psychology and Psychotherapy: Theory, Research and Practice*, 84(1), 98–110.

Fonagy, P., Steele, M. and Steele, H. (1991). The capacity for understanding mental states: The reflective self in parent and child and its significance for security of attachment. *Infant Mental Health Journal*, 12, 201–218.

Fonagy, P., Steele, M., Steele, H., Higgitt, A. and Target, M. (1994). The theory and practice of resilience. *Journal of Child Psychology and Psychiatry*, 35, 231–257.

Frankl, V. E. (1967). *Psychotherapy and Existentialism: Selected Papers on Logotherapy*. London: Penguin.

Freud, S. (1900). *The Interpretation of Dreams*. New York: Basic Books Inc.

Freud, S. (1912). *Recommendations to Physicians Practising Psycho-Analysis,* Standard Edition,. London: Hogarth Press.

Freud, S. (1930). *Civilisation and its Discontents,* Standard Edition. London: Hogarth Press.

Galin, D. (1974). Implications for psychiatry of left and right cerebral specialisation. *Archives of General Psychiatry*, 31, 572–583.

Gaussen, T. (2001). Dynamic Systems Theory: Revolutionising Developmental Psychology. *Irish Journal of Psychology*, 22, 3–4, 160–175.

Gardner, R. (1998). The brain and communication are basic for clinical human sciences. *British Journal of Medical Psychology*, 71(4), 493–508.

Gebser, J. (1986). *The Ever-present Origin* (Authorized translation by Noel Barstad with Algis Mickunas). Athens, OH: Ohio University Press.

Gee, H. (2000). La génétique et l'embryologie volent au secours de Darwin. *Le Monde*, Sciences, p. 26, 25th February.

Gibson, M. (1995). *Symbolism*. Cologne: Taschen Verlag.

Gilbert, P. (1995). Power, social rank and depression: Comments on Price and Gardner. *British Journal of Medical Psychology*, 68(3), 211–215.

Gilbert, P. (1998a). Evolutionary psychopathology: Why isn't mind designed better than it is? *British Journal of Medical Psychology*, 71(4), 353–373.

Gilbert, P. (1998b). The evolved basis and adaptive functions of cognitive distortion. *British Journal of Medical Psychology*, 71(4), 447–463.

Gould, S. J. (1977). *Ever Since Darwin: Reflections in Natural History*. New York: W. W. Norton.

Gould, S. J. (2002). *The Structure of Evolutionary Theory*. Harvard: Harvard University Press.

Graves, C. W. (2005). The Never Ending Quest. Eds. C. C. Cowan and Todorovic, N. Santa Barbara: ECLET Publishing.

Gribbin, J. (1999). *The Birth of Time: How We Measure the Age of the Universe*, London: Weidenfeld and Nicolson.

Griffin, D. (2001). Loss as a lifelong regenerative learning process. *Psychodynamic Counselling*, 7(4), 413–430.

Grof, S. (1975). *Realms of the Human Unconscious*. London: Souvenir Press.

Guenancia, P. (2009). L'événement du dualism. *Philosophie*, 31, 44–45.

Halpin, M. (Ed.) (2014). *How to be Happy and Healthy – the Seven Natural Elements of Mental Health*. Dublin: Ashfield Press.

Harari, Y. N. (2014). *Sapiens: A Brief History of Humankind*. London: Harvill Secker.

Harari, Y. N. (2015). *Homo Deus: A brief History of Tomorrow*. London: Harvill Secker.

Hayes, S. C. and Smith, S. (2005). *Get out of your Mind and into your Life: The New Acceptance and Commitment Therapy*. New York: Harbinger Publications.

Heide, F. T. and Borkovec, T. D. (1983). Paradoxical anxiety enhancement due to relaxation training. *Journal of Consulting and Clinical Psychology*, 51, 171–182.

Heide, F. T. and Borkovec, T. D. (1984). Relaxation-induced anxiety: Mechanisms and theoretical implications. *Behavior Research and Therapy,* 22, 1–12.

Heimann, P. (1950). On counter-transference. *International Journal of Psychoanalysis,* 31, 81–84.

Heimann, P. (1960). Counter-transference. In *About Children and Children-No-Longer.* Margaret Tonnesmann (Ed.), London: Routledge.

Hendricks, C. C. (1975). Meditation as discrimination training: A theoretical note. *Journal of Transpersonal Psychology*, 7 (2), 144–146.

Hillesum, E. (1986). *Het Verstoorde Leven (The Disturbed Life)*. Amsterdam: Balans Publishers.

Hogan, C. C. (1995). *Psychosomatics, Psychoanalysis and Inflammatory Disease of the Colon*. Madison, Connecticut: International Universities Press.

Hogan, M. J. (2008). On spirituality: Deconstructing, grappling, and moving in the field of others. *The Irish Psychologist,* 34(7), 187–197.

Holmes, J. (1997). Attachment, autonomy, intimacy: Some clinical implications of attachment theory. *British Journal of Medical Psychology*, 70(3), 231–248.

James, O. (2007). Selfish capitalism and mental illness. *The Psychologist*, 20(7), 426–428.

James, W. (1902). *The Variety of Religious Experience*. New York: Penguin Classics.

Jaspers, K. (1965). *The Origin and Goal of History*. New Haven, Massachusetts: Yale University Press.

Jung, C. G. (1958). Psychological commentary on the Tibetan book of the great liberation. In *Psychology and Religion, Vol.2, Collected Works*. New York: Pantheon Books.

Jung, C. G. (1958a). The transcendent function. In *Collected Works, Vol.* 8, London: Routledge and Kegan Paul.

Jung, C. G. (1958b). *Psychology and Religion: West and East,* Collected Works, Vol. 1. New York: Pantheon Books.

Jung, C. G. (1964). *Man and His Symbols*. London: Aldus Books.

Jung, C. G. (1971a). *Psychological Types*. Revised by R. F. C. Hull, Vol. 6, Collected Works, New Jersey: Princeton University Press.

Jung, C. G. (1971b). *Definitions. Collected Works,* Vol. 6. New York: Pantheon Books, pp. 473–476.

Kabat-Zinn, J. (1996). Mindfulness meditation: What it is, what it isn't, and its role in health-care and medicine. In Y. Haruki, Y. Ishii and M. Suzuki (Eds.), *Comparative and Psychological Study of Meditation*. Delft: The Netherlands, Eburon Publishers, pp. 161–170.

Kabat-Zinn, J. (2005). *Coming to our Senses: Healing ourselves and the World through Mindfulness*. New York: Hyperion.

Keinanen, M. (1998). The meaning of symbolic function in psycho-analytic psychotherapy: Clinical theory and psychotherapeutic applications. *British Journal of Medical Psychology*, 70 (4), 325–338.

Kelly, G. A. (1955). *The Psychology of Personal Constructs*. New York: Norton.

Kelly, T. (2007). Individuation in a consumer society: Acquiring versus becoming. Paper presented by the Irish Analytical Psychology Association, Trinity College, Dublin, 20th April.

Kenny, V. and DelMonte, M. M. (1986). Meditation as viewed through Personal Construct Theory. *Journal of Contemporary Psychotherapy*, 16(1), 4–22.

Keogh, C., Barnes-Holmes, Y. and Barnes-Holmes, D. (2008). Fused or de-fused? Getting to grips to what your mind is telling you. *The Irish Psychologist*, 35(1), 1–8.

Khan, M. (1977). On lying fallow: An aspect of leisure. *International Journal of Psychoanalytic Psychotherapy*, 6, 397–402.

Klein, M. (1928). Early stages of the Oedipus conflict. In *Love, Guilt and Reparation and Other Works 1921–1945*, pp. 186–198. London: Vintage, 1998.

Klein, M. (1946a). *Envy and Gratitude*. London: Virago.

Klein, M. (1946b). Notes on some schizoid mechanisms. In *Envy and Gratitude*. London: Virago, pp.1–24.

Kohn, M. (2004). *A Reason for Everything: Natural Selection and the English Imagination*. London: Faber and Faber.

Kohut, H. (1977). *The Restoration of the Self*. New York: International University Press.

Kretschmer, W. (1962). Meditation techniques in psychotherapies. *Psychologia*, 5, 76–83.

Krishnamurti, J. (1991). *Meeting life: Writing and Talks on Finding your Path without Retreating from Society*. San Francisco: Harper.

Lacan, J. (1966). *Ecrits*. Paris: Seuil.

Langs, R. and Badalamenti, A. (1996). *The Cosmic Circle: The Unification of Mind, Matter and Energy*. New York: Alliance Publishing Inc.

Leader, D. and Corfield, D. (2008). *Why Do People Get Ill?* London: Penguin Books.

Lerner, H. (1989). *The Dance of Intimacy: A Woman's Guide to Courageous Acts of Change in Key Relationships*. New York: Harper and Row.

Lestel, D. (2003). *Les Origines Animales de la Culture*. Paris: Flammarion.

Lindahl, B. I. B. (1997). Consciousness and biological evolution. *Journal of Theoretical Biology*, 187, 613–629.

Liotti, G. and Gilbert, P. (2011). Mentalizing, motivation, and social mentalities: Theoretical considerations and implications for psychotherapy. *Psychology and Psychotherapy: Theory, Research and Practice,* 84 (1), 9–25. London: Routledge.

Lorenz, K. (1966). *On Aggression*. Norfolk: Cox and Wyman.

Lovelock, J. (2000). *A New Look at Life on Earth (3rd Edition)*. Oxford: Oxford University Press.

Main, J. (1982). *Letters from the Heart*. New York: Crossroads.

Main, J. (1984). *Moment of Christ: The Path of Meditation*. London: Darton, Longman and Todd.

Main, J. (1989). *The Way of Unknowing*. London: Darton, Longman.

Marx Hubbard, B. (2015). *Conscious Evolution: Awakening the Power of Our Social Potential. California: New World Library; Revised Edition*.

Mascaro, J. (1962). *The Bhagavad Gita*. London: Penguin.

Matte Blanco, I. (1988). *Thinking, Feeling and Being*. London: Routledge.

Maslow, A. H. (1968). *Toward a Psychology of Being*. New York: Van Nostrand.

Matthews, R. (2005). *25 Big Ideas: The Science that is Changing our World*. London: One World Publications.

Maturana, H. (1978). Biology of Language: The Epistemology of Reality. In Miller, G. and Lenneberg, E. (Eds.), *Psychology and Biology of Language and Thought*. New York: Academic Press.

Maynard Smith, J. (1966). *The Theory of Evolution*. London: Penguin.

McClintock, B. (1961). Some parallels between gene control systems in maize and bacteria. *The American Naturalist*, 95(884), 265–277.

McDougall, W. (1921). *The Group Mind: A Sketch of the Principles of Collective Psychology with Some Attempt to Apply Them to the Interpretation of National Life and Character.* Cambridge: Cambridge University Press.

McGee, D., Browne, I., Kenny, V., McGennis, A., and Pilot, J. (1984). Unexperienced experience: A critical reappraisal of the theory of regression and traumatic neurosis. *Irish Journal of Psychotherapy.* 3(1), 7–19.

McGuire, M. T. and Troisi, A. (1998). Prevalence differences in depression among males and females: Are there evolutionary explanations? *British Journal of Medical Psychology*, 71(4), 479–491.

McWilliams, S. A. (1984). Construing and Buddhist psychology, *Constructs*, 3(1), 1–2.

Meares, A. (1978). Vivid visualisation and dim visual awareness in the regression of cancer in meditation. *Journal of the American Society of Psychosomatic Dentistry and Medicine.* 25(3), 85–88.

Mendoza, S. (2010). The O of emptiness and the emptiness of O. *British Journal of Psychotherapy*, 26(3), 305–320.

Méry, F. (1971). *Les Bêtes Aussi Ont Leur Langages.* Paris, Editions France-Empire.

Michalak, J., Holz, A. and Teismann, T. (2011). Rumination as a predictor of relapse in mindfulness-based cognitive therapy for depression. *Psychology and Psychotherapy: Theory, Research and Practice*, 84(2), 230–236.

Mitchell, S. A. (1998). Attachment theory and the psychoanalytic tradition: Reflections on human relationality. *British Journal of Psychotherapy*, (2), 177–193.

Moncayo, R. (2003). The finger pointing at the moon: Zen practice and the practice of Lacanian psychoanalysis. In J. D. Sanfran (Ed.), *Psychoanalysis and Buddhism: An Unfolding Dialogue.* New York: Wisdom Publishers.

Nesse, P. (1998). Emotional disorders in evolutionary perspective. *British Journal of Medical Psychology*, 71(4), 397–415.

Nino, A. G. (1997). Assessment of spiritual quests in clinical practice. *International Journal of Psychotherapy*, 2(2), 193–212.

Noble, D. (2006). *The Music of Life: Biology beyond Genes.* Oxford: Oxford University Press.

Noble, D. (2011). Neo-Darwinism, the Modern Synthesis, and selfish genes: Are they of use in physiology? *Journal of Physiology*, 589, 1007–1015.

Norton, S. R., Rhodes, L. and Hauch, J. (1985). Characteristics of subjects experiencing relaxation and relaxation-induced anxiety. *Journal of Behaviour Therapy and Experimental Psychiatry*, 16, 211–216.

O'Brien, E. (1964). *The Essential Plotinus.* New York: Mentor.

O'Connor, L. E., Berry, J. W., Weiss, J., Schweitzer, D. and Senier, M. (2000). Survivor guilt, submissive behaviour and evolutionary theory: The down-side of winning in social competition. *British Journal of Medical Psychology*, 73(4), 519–530.

O'Donoghue, J. (1997). *Anam Cara: Spiritual Wisdom of the Celtic World.* London: Bantam Press.

Oatley, K. (1992). *Best Laid Schemes: The Psychology of Emotions*. Cambridge: Cambridge University Press.

Passera, L. (2006). *La Véritable Histoire des Fourmis*. Paris: Fayard.

Pelled, E. (2007). Learning from experience: Bion's concept of reverie and Buddhist meditation. A comparative study. *International Journal of Psychoanalysis*, 88, 1507–1526.

Penrose, R. and Hameroff, S. (2011). Consciousness in the universe: Neuroscience, quantum space-time geometry and Orch OR theory. *Journal of Cosmology*, 14, 4421–4440.

Perls, F. S., Hefferline, R. F. and Goodman, P. (1973). *Gestalt Therapy: Excitement and Growth in the Human Personality*. London: Penguin.

Pert, C. (1998). The Matter of Mind: Emotions as the mind-body connection. In M. M. DelMonte and Y. Haruki (Eds.), *The Embodiment of Mind: Eastern and Western Perspectives*. Delft: Eburon Publishers.

Pert, C. (1999). *Molecules of Emotion: The Science behind Mind-Body Medicine*. New York: Schuster.

Piaget, J. (1967). *The Psychology of Intelligence*, London: Routledge Kegan Paul.

Picq, P., Sagart, L., Dehaene, G. and Lestienne, C. (2008). *La Plus Belle Histoire du Langage*. Paris: Seuil.

Pinker, S. (1994). *The Language Instinct*. London: Penguin Books.

Pinker, S. (1997). *How the Mind Works*. London: Penguin.

Pinker, S. (2002). *The Blank Slate*. London: Allen Lane Penguin Books.

Plato, in Benjamin Jowett's (1888) translation, *The Republic of Plato, Book (VI)*. Oxford: Clarendon Press.

Plomin, R. (2001). Genetics and behaviour. *The Psychologist*, 14(3), 134–139.

Polanyi, M. (1959). *The Study of Man*. Chicago: University of Chicago Press.

Popper, K. R. (1959). *The Logic of Scientific Discovery*, London: Hutchinson.

Price, J. (1998). The adaptive function of mood change. *British Journal of Medical Psychology*, 71(4), 465–477.

Price, J. and Gardner, R. (1995). The paradoxical power of the depressed patient: A problem for the ranking theory of depression. *British Journal of Medical Psychology*, 68(3), 193–206.

Prigogine, I. and Stengers, I. (1984). *Order out of Chaos*. London: William Heinemann. process. *Psychodynamic Counselling*, 7(4), 413–430.

Ramseyer, F. and Tschacher, W. (2006). Synchrony: A core concept for a constructivist approach to psychotherapy. *Constructivism in the Human Sciences*, 11(1), 150–171.

Reeves, H. (2005). *Chroniques du Ciel et de la Vie*. Paris: Editions du Seuil.

Reeves, H. (2011). *Origins: Speculations on the Cosmos, Earth and Mankind*. New York: Skyhorse Publishing Company.

Reid, S. (1990). The importance of beauty in the psychoanalytic experience. *Journal of Child Psychotherapy*, 16A, 29–52.

Reville, W. (1996). Science Today. *The Irish Times*, 9th September, Dublin.

Reville, W. (2006). Science Today. *The Irish Times*, 2nd March, Dublin.

Robinson, K. (2006). How Schools Kill Creativity. TED Talk, http://www.ted.com/talks/ ken_robinson_says_schools_kill_creativity.

Rubin, J. B. (1985). Meditation and psychoanalytic listening. *Psychoanalytic Review*, 72(4), 599–613.

Russell, E. W. (1986). Consciousness and the unconscious: Eastern meditative and Western therapeutic approaches. *Journal of Transpersonal Psychology*, 18(1), 51–72.

Ryle, A. (1994). Projective identification: A particular form of reciprocal role procedure, *British Journal of Medical Psychology*, 67, 107–114.

Ryle, A. (2005). The relevance of evolutionary psychology for psychotherapy. *British Journal of Psychotherapy*, 21(3), 375–388.

Sahtouris, E. (2000). *Earth Dance: Living Systems in Evolution*. Lincoln: iUniverse.

Schore, A. N. (1994). *Affect Regulation and the Origin of the Self: The Neurobiology of Emotional Development*. New Jersey: Lawrence Erlbaum, Hillsdale.

Schore, A. N. (2001). Minds in the Making: Attachment, the self-organizing brain, and developmentally oriented psychoanalytic psychotherapy, *British Journal of Psychotherapy*, 17(3), 299–328.

Schore, A. N. (2003). The Seventh Annual John Bowlby Memorial Lecture: Minds in the making. In J. Corrigall and H. Wilkinson (Eds.), *Revolutionary Connections: Psychotherapy and Neuroscience* (pp. 7–51). London and New York: Karnac.

Schwartz, G. E. (1983). Disregulation theory and disease: Applications to repression/ cerebral disconnection/cardiovascular disorder hypothesis. *International Review of Applied Psychology*, 32, 95–118.

Schwartz, J. (2000). Review essay: A beginner's guide to the brain. Ten lectures on the neurology of mental life. Mark Solms at the Anna Freud Centre. *British Journal of Psychotherapy*, 17(2), 173–179.

Semrud-Clikeman, M. and Hynd, G. W. (1990). Right hemisphere dysfunction in non-verbal learning disabilities: social, academic and adaptive functioning in adults and children. *Psychological Bulletin*, 107,196–209.

Shafii, M. (1973a). Silence in the service of the ego: Psychoanalytic study of meditation. *International Journal of Psycho-Analysis*, 54(4), 431–443.

Shafii, M. (1973b). Adaptive and therapeutic aspects of meditation. *International Journal of Psychoanalytic Psychotherapy*, 2, 364–382.

Sheldrake, R. (1988). *The Presence of the Past*. London: Harper-Collins.

Skinner, B. F. (1971). *Beyond Freedom and Dignity*. London: Penguin Books.

Song, T. (1998). *History of Qi-gong*. Paper presented at the 5th Conference of the Transnational Network for the Study of Physical, Psychological and Spiritual Well-being, April 1998, Beijing, China.

Speeth, K. R. (1982). On therapeutic attention. *Journal of Transpersonal Psychology*, 14(2), 141–160.

Stevens, A. and Price, J. (1996). *Evolutionary Psychiatry: A New Beginning*. London: Routledge.

Sthalekar, H. (2000). Hypnosis in the past, present and in the New Millennium. *Australian Journal of Clinical Hypnotherapy and Hypnosis*, 21(2), pp. 65–80.

Storr, A. (1965). *Sexual Deviation*. London: Heinemann.

Storr, A. (1972). *The Dynamics of Creation*. London: Penguin.

Storr, A. (1992). *Music and the Mind,* London: Harper Collins.

Streit, J. (1984). *Sun and Cross*. Edinburgh: Floris Books.

Suler, J. R. (1991). The T'ai Chi images: A Taoist model of psychotherapeutic change. *Psychologia*, 34, 18–27.

Szasz, T. S. (1972a). *The Myth of Mental Illness*. London: Paladin.

Szasz, T. S. (1972b). A psychologist's experience with Transcendental Meditation. *Journal of Transpersonal Psychology*, 3, 135–140.

Teasdale, J. (2000). A mindfulness-based cognitive therapy for prevention of relapse and recurrence in major depression. Paper read at the 6th conference of the Transnational Network for the Study of Physical, Psychological and Spiritual Well-being, Noordwijkerhout, The Netherlands.

Teilhard de Chardin, P. (1950/1976). *The Heart of Matter*. USA: Williams Collins and Sons.

Teilhard de Chardin, P. (1959) *The Phenomenon of Man* (Translated by Bernard Wall). London: William Collins and Sons.

Thich Nhat Hanh (1975). *The Miracle of Mindfulness*. London: Rider.

Thich Nhat Hanh, (1987). *Interbeing: Fourteen Guidelines for Engaged Buddhism*. Berkeley: Parallax Press.

Thich Nhat Hanh (1991). *Peace is Every Step: The Path of Mindfulness in Everyday Life*. London: Rider.

Thich Nhat Hanh (2003). *Creating True Peace: Ending Conflict in Yourself, Your Family, Your Community and the World*. London: Rider.

Thompson, W. I. (1981). *The Time Falling Bodies Take to Light: Mythology, Sexuality and the Origins of Culture*. New York: St Martin's Press.

Thompson, W. I. (2001). *Transforming History: A Curriculum for Cultural Evolution*. USA: Lindisfarne Books.

Thwaites, R. and Dagnan, D. (2004). Moderating variables in the relationship between social comparison and depression: An evolutionary perspective. *Psychology and Psychotherapy: Theory, Research and Practice,* 77, 309–323.

Tinbergen, N. (1965). *Social Behaviour in Animals*. London: Science Paperbacks.

Todorov, T. (1996). *L'homme Dépaysé*. Paris: Editions du Seuil.

Tolle, E. (1999). *The Power of Now*. Novato, California: New World Library.

Tolle, E. (2005). *A New Earth: Awakening to your Life's Purpose*. London: Penguin Group.

Trinh Xuan Thuan. (2011). *Le Cosmos et le Lotus*. Paris: Editions Albin Michel.

Troop, N. A; Allan, S; Treasure, J. L. and Katzman, M. (2003). Social comparison and submissive behaviour in eating disorder patients. *Psychology and Psychotherapy: Theory, Research and Practice*, 76, 237–249.

Van der Kolk, B. and Fisher, R. (1995). Dissociation and the fragmentary nature of traumatic memories: Overview and explanatory study. *Journal of Traumatic Stress*, 8, 505–525.

Van Lommel, P. (2010). *Consciousness beyond Life: The Science of the Near Death Experience*. New York: Harper Collins Publishers.

Vanheule, S., Vandenbergen, J., Verhaeghe, P., and Desmet, M. (2010). Interpersonal Problems in alexithymia: A study in three primary care groups. *Psychology and Psychotherapy: Theory, Research and Practice, 83*(4), 351–362.

Vanheule, S., Verhaeghe, P. and Desmet, M. (2011). In search of a framework in the treatment of alexithymia. *Psychology and Psychotherapy: Theory, Research and Practice, 84*(1), 84–97.

Varela, F. J. and Maturana, H. (1981). Living warp of sense-making: A middle path for neuroscience. Paper presented at the International Symposium on Disorder and Order, Stanford University, Palo Alto, California.

Vernadsky, V. (1943/2005). Some Words about the Noösphere. *21st Century Science and Technology, Vol. 18, No 1, Spring 2005*.

Von Bertalanffy, L. (1968). *General Systems Theory*. New York: Brazillier.

Vygotsky, L. (1978). In M. Cole, V. John-Steiner, S. Scriber and E. Souberman (Eds.). *Mind in Society: The Development of Higher Psychological Processes*. Cambridge, MA: Harvard University Press.

Wagner, A. (2014). *Arrival of the Fittest: Solving Evolution's Greatest Puzzle*. New York: Current.

Wallace, A. R. (1870). The limits of natural selection as applied to man. In *Contributions to the Theory of Natural Selection; A Selection of Essays*. London: Macmillan and Co.

Wallace, A. R. (1895). The expressiveness of speech, or mouth-gesture as a factor in the origin of language. *Fortnightly Review*, 58 (n.s.): 528–543.

Walsh, R. and Shapiro, S. L. (2006). The meeting of meditative disciplines and Western Psychology: A mutually enriching dialogue. *American Psychologist, 61*(3), 227–239.

Wang, W. (1998). Study of the psychology and the behavioral science of Qigong. In M. DelMonte and Y. Haruki (Eds.), *The Embodiment of Mind: Eastern and Western Perspectives*. Delft: The Netherlands, Eburon Publishers.

Warrenburg, S., Crits-Christoph, P. and Schwartz, G. E. (1981). Biobehavioral etiology and treatment of hypertension: A comparative outcome study of stress management and diet change approaches. Paper presented at the NATO Symposium on Behavioural Medicine, Greece, July.

Watts, A. W. (1957). *The Way of Zen*. Harmondsworth, Middlesex: Penguin.

Weber, A. (2016). *The Biology of Wonder: Aliveness, Feeling and the Metamorphosis of Science*. Gabriola Island BC, Canada: New Society Publishers.

Wickrama-Singh, C. (2001). "We are all aliens". Paper presented at the Cork Institute of Technology, Cork, 12th October.

Wilber, K. (1996). *Up from Eden: A Transpersonal View of Human Development*, New York: Quest Books.

Wilber, K. (2000). *Integral Psychology: Consciousness, Spirit, Psychology, Therapy*. Boston, Massachusetts: Shambhala.

Wilber, K. (2008). *Integral Life Practice: A 21st-Century Blueprint for Physical Health, Emotional Balance, Mental Clarity, and Spiritual Awakening*. Massachusetts: Integral Books.

Wilber, K., Engler, J., Brown, D. (1991).*Transformations of Consciousness: Conventional and Contemplative Perspectives on Development*. New York: Shambhala Publications Inc.

Wilson, D. R. (1998). Evolutionary epidemiology and manic depression. *British Journal of Medical Psychology*, 71(4), 375–395.

Winnicott, D. (1971). *Playing and Reality*. London: Tavistock.

Wohlleben, P. (2016). *The Hidden Life of Trees: What they Feel and How they Communicate*. Vancouver, Canada: Greystone Books.

Womack, M. (2005). *Symbols and Meaning: A Concise Introduction*. California: AltaMira Press.

Wright, K. (1998). Deep calling unto deep: Artistic creativity and the maternal object. *British Journal of Psychotherapy*, 14(4), 453–467.

Yoon, C. K. (2007). From a few genes, life's many forms. New York: *The New York Times*, 30th June.

Zimmer, H. (1969). J. Campbell (Ed.). *Philosophies of India*. Princeton: Princeton University Press.

Name and Subject Index

Author Index